Foreign Advertising in

China

Foreign Advertising in China

Becoming Global, Becoming Local

JIAN WANG

Iowa State University Press / Ames

Jian Wang is a communications specialist in the Hong Kong office of McKinsey & Company. He has been an assistant professor of journalism and communication at the Chinese University of Hong Kong. Dr. Wang received a B.A. in English from Beijing University, an M.A. in journalism and mass communication from the University of Minnesota, and a Ph.D. in mass communications from the University of Iowa.

Iowa State University Press
2121 South State Avenue, Ames, Iowa 50014

Orders:	1-800-862-6657
Office:	1-515-292-0140
Fax:	1-515-292-3348
Web site:	www.isupress.edu

First edition, 2000

Library of Congress Cataloging-in-Publication Data
Wang, Jian
Foreign advertising in China : becoming global, becoming local / Jian Wang—1st ed.
p. cm.
Includes bibliographical references and index.
ISBN 0-8138-1828-1
1. Advertising—China. 2. International business enterprises—China.
3. Investments, Foreign—China. I. Title.

HF5813.C5 W36 2000
659.1'0951—dc21 00-026811

The last digit is the print number: 9 8 7 6 5 4 3 2 1

To my parents

Contents

Acknowledgments

This book is based on a dissertation I wrote at the University of Iowa in 1997. I am grateful for the intellectual and financial support I received at the University of Iowa. My warmest thanks to Kenneth Starck, Judy Polumbaum, Carol Fethke, John Soloski, and Hanno Hardt for their guidance during my dissertation research. My research was generously supported by a T. Anne Cleary International Dissertation Research Award, a John F. Murray Dissertation Scholarship, and a Center for Asian and Pacific Studies Dissertation Grant.

As I continued working on the manuscript while teaching at the Chinese University of Hong Kong, I also received from the Chinese University a Direct Grant for Research, which allowed me to study the archival materials at the Western Historical Manuscript Collection of the University of Missouri at Columbia.

I benefited greatly from many stimulating conversations with Zhang Ximin, who is never short of enthusiasm and insight and is always helpful. Xu Kai and Qiu Lin-chuan were such able and thoughtful research assistants. During different stages of this project, Chang Hong, Sun Xupei, and Li Hairong also provided me with much needed help in various ways. I am also grateful for the encouragement and direction I received from Tsan-Kuo Chang of the University of Minnesota, where I began my graduate studies.

Thanks to the dozens of advertising professionals and scholars in China, named or unnamed in the following pages, for their goodwill and for taking the time to share with me information and insights about the industry. A special thank you to the late Xu Baiyi, the "grand old man" of Chinese advertising. I was fortunate to have interviewed him on several occasions in 1996 and 1997. Mr. Xu provided me with a valuable history of advertising development in China and, better, with a sense of history. He generously shared with me his unpublished manuscripts, which afforded me a rare glimpse into the advertising content and practice in Shanghai in the 1930s and 1940s. Despite poor health and advanced age, he continued writing about Chinese advertising, working tirelessly in his modest apartment in Shanghai. I was most humbled and truly inspired by his remarkable dedication and perseverance.

I owe special thanks to David McElwee, whose unfailing support in reading the manuscript with care and understanding helped me see the project through to completion.

I express my appreciation to Judi Brown, Anne Bolen, and Iowa State University Press for their interest in my proposal and their support.

Portions of the manuscript are revisions of previously published articles: "From four hundred million to more than one billion consumers: A brief history of the foreign advertising industry in China," *International Journal of Advertising* 16 (4), 1997; "Through the looking-glass of foreign ads in China," *Asian Journal of Communication* 17 (1), 1997; "Global media and cultural change," *Media Asia* 24 (1), 1997; and "The siren songs of consumption: An analysis of foreign advertisements in two Mainland Chinese newspapers, 1985-1993," *Gazette* 56 (3), 1996. Permissions for their use are gratefully acknowledged. In addition, parts of Chapter 2 are reprinted with the permission of Fitzroy Dearborn Publishers.

Finally, profound gratitude goes to my parents and other family members whose love, understanding, and encouragement have helped sustain me and cheer me on.

Foreign Advertising in

China

1

China's Encounter with Global Advertising Culture

Spring 1996.

At the heart of China's capital city, Beijing, stands a huge electronic roadside billboard. Displayed on the billboard are three "heroes"—a Caucasian man, a Caucasian woman, and a Hennessy bottle set against the backdrop of a peaceful blue sea. The dark-suited man, glass in hand, is posed in the middle of the background. In the left foreground, barely visible in the scene, the woman is showing only a shoulder draped in a beautiful scarf. On the right is the big Hennessy bottle, with its shape and texture occupying almost a quarter of the billboard space. Between the back and the front is a row of Greco-Roman arches. The ad caption written in Chinese characters reads, "Hennessy. The Original X.O."

A moment later the billboard dissolves into a slightly different setting featuring a curved white verandah overlooking the quiet blue sea. Standing on the verandah, the Caucasian man, gazing seaward and still holding a glass, is now impeccably attired in a white tropical suit. The Caucasian woman now appears in a high-cut white dress, but only her back from hip to shoulder is shown. She also is looking out to sea. The Hennessy bottle remains prominent, unaltered from its original position on the right side of the billboard.

Once again, in a slow dissolve, the billboard magically transforms itself into a third and final tableau. Now coming into view is a public service poster covered with twenty big and bold white Chinese characters written against a red backdrop with floral decorations on either side. The slogan, consisting of five four-word phrases, translates literally as "Seizing opportunity, deepening reform, broadening open policy, promoting development, maintaining stability." On the lower right side appears the credit of the "Propaganda Department of Beijing Municipal Committee of the Chinese Communist Party."

Embodying the essence of Western advertising—subtle and sophisticated—the Hennessy ads depict a surreal world of elegance, romance, sexuality, high class, escapism, and the exotic. The local public service ad, on the other hand, manifests the ethos of Chinese political propaganda—simplistic and straightforward. These advertising posters are of different "aesthetic sensibility" and "emotional intensity," to borrow Michael Schudson's concept of capitalist as opposed to socialist realism. The Hennessy ads are upscale, cool, "sentimental, and appealing openly to the basic human feeling," whereas the public service ad is public-spirited, hot, "emotionally overextended, tugging toward inspiration."[1]

Amidst the hustle and bustle of downtown Beijing, upon this giant electronic billboard is where capitalist realism meets socialist realism and the global meets the local. The sequential flow of the disparate advertising imagery serves as a daily reminder of the cultural contrasts and contradictions in contemporary China.

After the Cold War came the Cola War. Indeed, the Cola War has also broken out on the Chinese front. In summer 1995 Coca-Cola placed its posters on top of public newspaper reading cases along Chang An Avenue in Beijing. Coke's presence on China's

First Boulevard is of no little symbolic significance. It did not take long before Pepsi-Cola decorated the bus-stop kiosks along the same avenue with its red and blue logos. One culmination of the Cola War occurred in November of that same year when Coke quietly erected its biggest billboard in China on top of the office tower where Pepsi's Beijing office was located. Coke claimed another symbolic victory over Pepsi in its drive to conquer the emerging soft-drink market in China.

The world's economy has become "stateless" and "borderless."[2] "For the first time in human history," declared economist Lester G. Thurow, "anything can be made anywhere and sold everywhere."[3] The evolving globalization of industrial and service enterprises includes and depends on the globalization of advertising business. Under a hospitable climate and with the promise of profit making, ad agencies follow their clients to business frontiers around the world. As the world's most populous nation and the world's largest potential consumer market, China cannot be ignored.

In the early 1960s less than one-fifth of the total worldwide billings of the 10 largest U.S. ad agencies were generated from overseas markets; but by the end of the 1980s the share of overseas billings had risen to 54%.[4] For the top 500 U.S.-based ad agencies, their overseas share in the worldwide income grew from less than 25% (US$2.15 billion) in 1986 to more than 40% (US$7.15 billion) in 1995.[5] The ad agency Young & Rubicam has established a global network of over 300 offices, spanning from Asia and Africa to Europe and the Americas. As Armand Mattelart has put it, "The question of advertising has long ceased to be a national question. . . ."[6]

In 1992 the International Monetary Fund rated China as the third largest economy in the world, trailing only the United States and Japan. Some have reservations about such statistics concerning China's economic power. One article in *The Economist* suggested that China's poverty is more widespread than what has been presented and projected.[7] It is also a fact that despite the enormous size of its economy, with a population of more than 1.3 billion, China's per capita income still lags far behind the more-developed countries. Nonetheless, China's economic development in the last decade has been consistent and impressive. The remarkable and persistent rise in people's disposable income and their standard of living since the country adopted economic reform policies in the late 1970s is indisputable. Such economic growth has also awakened Chinese people's consumption desires. Chinese consumers have started to aspire to acquire Western brand-name products and emulate Western consumption behavior.[8] The emergence of a consumer culture in China is beyond anyone's doubt. As Orville Schell observed, during the pre-reform era "all Chinese were supposed to dedicate themselves heart and soul to the task of building revolutionary socialism" rather than enjoying themselves "as if non-political fun were an inalienable right."[9] It is truly a cultural revolution in and of itself when the notion of seeking material pleasures and "having fun" has become accepted in the Chinese society.

Global corporations did not waste any time in entering the Chinese market when China's doors were reopened to the West in the late 1970s, and it has since participated in China's economic boom with energy and enthusiasm. The almost mythical prospect of selling in the potential market of more than one billion consumers is simply irresistible. As a report in *The Economist* described,[10]

> The purveyors of nearly all the world's big consumer brands are battling for at least a foothold in the Chinese market. Pizza Hut, Kentucky Fried Chicken, and McDonald's serve up fast food. Chinese consumers are wooed by Cadbury's chocolate, biscuits from United Biscuits, Maxwell House coffee from Kraft General Foods, and Knorr bouillon cubes from America's CPC. Smokers are tempted by advertisements for Marlboro, Salem, and Lucky Strike cigarettes. Drinkers are invited to open a can of beer from Australia's Fosters, Denmark's Carlsberg, or the Philippines' San Miguel. Department stores offer Estée Lauder cosmetics, shoes from London's Gieves & Hawkes, and Louis Vuitton handbags.

General Motors, Ford, Toyota, and other global car makers are making their way into the unexplored Chinese auto market.[11] AT&T competes with Japanese, German, and French companies to build the information superhighway in China.[12] Microsoft officially launched its Chinese Windows 95 in the Forbidden City of Beijing in March 1996 even though counterfeit copies had by then been widely available in the streets.[13]

In Shanghai, the Japanese retail giant Kazuo Wada opened its Nextage department store, the second largest in the world (only behind Macy's Herald Square in Manhattan).[14] Another global retailer, Wal-Mart, had opened two stores in China by September 1996.[15] The largest Pepsi bottling plant in the Asian Pacific region was set up in China's most populous Sichuan province.[16]

Despite arguments that trace the roots of advertising to ancient China, modern advertising was only introduced to China at the turn of the century. Advertising first flourished in China's commercial center, Shanghai, during the 1920s and 1930s. Its development was interrupted when the Chinese Communist Party came into power and began to institute a central command economy in the 1950s. Commercial advertising later became irrelevant in the transformed Chinese socio-economic and media system, and eventually disappeared from the mass media. Its return in the late 1970s was the direct outcome of the market-oriented reform in post-Mao China. Advertising has since enjoyed tremendous growth. In the 10-year period from 1987 to 1996, ad spending in China increased by almost 900%, making the country the world's fastest growing advertising market.[17]

Foreign advertising entered China with the development of international businesses in the Chinese market.[18] In the early 1980s, the global advertising industry still viewed the Chinese market with "guarded optimism,"[19] but the cautious approach has since given way to expressed confidence in the bright prospects of the Chinese consumer wonderland. At the beginning of the 1990s there were only four joint-venture ad agencies in China, but by 1997 that number had grown to 433.[20] All the major players in global advertising have since set up shops there, representing a wide array of consumer product brands and manufacturers, from

Kodak and Coca-Cola to Panasonic and Procter & Gamble. Among the top 10 ad agencies in China in 1995, four were multinational agencies.[21] That year multinational advertising grew much faster than the Chinese domestic advertising sector (172.2% vs. 51.7%).[22] It is not surprising to note that two years later (in 1997), multinational agencies occupied seven spots in the top 10 category.[23]

The multinational ad agencies have also been successful in introducing and cultivating foreign brand names and images in the minds of Chinese consumers. The global consumer product manufacturers in China are reaping the rewards of advertising and promotion. A television commercial for Nestle coffee was one of the first astounding successes. In the early 1980s the Nestle slogan "The taste is excellent," spoken by a young man with a slightly southern China accent, quickly made its way into the Chinese vernacular (its popularity was comparable to Wendy's "Where's the beef?" slogan in the United States). Equally successful, as any schoolboy would tell you, Citizen was "leading the trend as always; leading quartz watch technology all over the world." In 1986 J. Walter Thompson launched an ad campaign for Lux beauty soap in Guangzhou, and the sales of Lux doubled within half a year.[24] Raid insecticide created high brand awareness in Shanghai in a short period of time with its well-coordinated ad campaign in 1991.[25] The 1994 Gallup survey of Chinese consumers (claimed to be the first nationwide consumer survey by a foreign research company) indicated that, in China, foreign brands had achieved much higher brand recognition than had domestic brands.[26] Of the top 10 brand-awareness leaders in the Chinese market, nine were foreign brands—Hitachi, Coca-Cola, Panasonic, Toyota, Mickey Mouse, Marlboro, Suzuki, and Honda. China's Tsingdao (beer) was the sole domestic entry.

Advertising, Consumption, and Culture

Consumer goods are communicative. They constitute sources of economic, social, and cultural information for our everyday life. "Instead of supposing that goods are primarily needed for subsistence plus competitive display," argued Mary Douglas and Baron Isherwood, "let us assume that they are needed for making visible and stable the categories of culture."[27] Goods are carriers of meaning; yet the meaning is not intrinsic in the product. Consumption is therefore the process by which these meanings are created and recreated.

Material consumption is both literal and figurative. It includes not only consumption of goods but also of ideas and images, especially those represented in advertising.[28] One of the prime purveyors of consumer culture is commercial advertising. Besides promoting and selling products and services, advertising tries to ascribe meaning and identity to goods. As James Twitchell has pointed out, "In giving value to objects, advertising gives value to our lives."[29] Advertising thus performs a cultural as well as an economic function. Even though the ubiquity of advertising in our daily life does not necessarily mean its "monopoly in the symbolic marketplace," advertising does possess "a special cultural power."[30]

Advertising has evolved from presenting simple, straightforward information about goods and services to representing a "choreographed" vision of life. It depicts not how we actually behave in our everyday life but how we think we should behave.[31] Raymond Williams observed that Western advertising has "passed the frontier of the selling of goods and services and has become involved with the teaching of social and personal values."[32] As Stuart Ewen also argued, we increasingly confront not the question of "what to buy" but of "what to dream."[33] The institution of advertising is, in a word, also a consciousness industry and a cultural apparatus.[34]

Foreign advertising opens a window on the world of capitalism for Chinese consumers. Through it, Chinese consumers are afforded a glimpse of modern consumer goods and lifestyles. As a focal point for interpretation in their encounter with global material culture, foreign advertising certainly intends to influence the buying habits of Chinese consumers as well as to orient their consumption behavior. In another sense, foreign advertising also possesses "news value." It provides Chinese consumers with a look at the idealized ways of life. It eventually turns into a form of social knowledge. As stated in an article in *Advertising Age International,* "It could be said that advertising and marketing can be a nation's unofficial diplomat overseas, representing a country's way of life more dramatically and realistically than official state department or foreign office ambassadors."[35] Even though its representations are carefully choreographed and highly stylized, foreign advertising, as social knowledge, is perhaps more informative and persuasive than the sights and sounds in daily news reports about aspects of the outside world. In the increasingly enlarged, complex, and variegated cultural and media environment in China, foreign advertising has become one special information source for the Chinese people, helping them imagine a better life.

In his study of the history of the U.S. agency N.W. Ayer & Son, Ralph M. Hower wrote,[36]

> To the majority of us advertising is the most familiar fact of modern business. Like the weather, it is always with us, and yet we seldom consciously observe it unless it is unusually good or bad. Nor do we often think about the underlying forces that produce it or consider fully the variety of results which flow from its use.

Although Hower made this observation more than half a century ago, there is still a grain of truth in it when we come to think about how little we understand advertising in contemporary society. As a field of study, foreign advertising in China has remained largely unexplored.

The omission is glaring. As the Chinese economy grows more open and diversified, the role of foreign advertising in China's social and cultural life cries out for examination. This book is concerned with the role of foreign advertising in China as a field of cultural production and consumption.

Advertising, Imperialism, and Globalization

The standard discourse in international communication research has long focused on Western advertising's deleterious impact on the cultures of Third World countries, of which China is a part.[37] Along with the Western/American entertainment establishment, multinational advertising has also been in the spotlight of the media/cultural imperialism controversy. It has often been criticized as a venture of Western imperialism or, more precisely, advertising imperialism for peddling and promoting Western consumer goods and ideals in the Third World, and for displacing local cultural values and traditions.[38] After World War II, with the rise of the United States as a political, economic, and military superpower and the concomitant decolonization in many parts of the world, the Western notion of modernization and development was widespread and accepted in the Third World. One important component of this modernization project was the development of modern mass media. Mass media were regarded as indispensable agencies for modernization in the newly independent countries.[39] The export of media technology, equipment, content, and professionalism from the West (mainly the United States) became prevalent and has remained crucial to media development in some countries.

But the optimism in the pursuit of modernization and development dissipated, later to be superseded by skepticism in the 1960s. Herbert Schiller propounded the concept of media/cultural imperialism in his book *Mass Communication and American Empire*.[40] He argued that the consequences of the expansion of U.S. media, economy and culture to other countries were the displacement of local traditions and the imposition of U.S. values onto other cultures.

The criticism of Western mass media expansion was echoed in the Third World. The height of the media and cultural imperialism debate was embodied by the New World Information and Communication Order (NWICO) movement in the 1970s, where Third World countries made concerted efforts to address and redress the uneven flow of information from the core capitalist countries to the peripheral developing countries. Amidst the Cold War the NWICO debate was highly politicized and fundamentally ideological. The withdrawal of the United States and Great Britain in the mid-1980s from the United Nations Educational,

Scientific and Cultural Organization, a major platform for NWICO, highlighted the clash between contending political ideologies and powers.

The passing of the Cold War era has found a relatively calm international political climate and the rapid development and dissemination of communications technology. Muhammadi Ayish identified two major global trends that are shaping the future of the world. First is the wide proliferation of modern communication and information technologies; second is the increasing democratization of social systems around the world in the wake of the disintegration of the former Soviet-led Communist block.[41] As a result, there is an unfolding third trend, which is the intensifying global expansion of primarily Western-based corporations. Against the backdrop of these interdependent developments, advertising expansion by the world's major corporations has also achieved a new momentum.

Does this new wave of media/advertising expansion smack of cultural imperialism? Is it a reincarnation of colonialism in media and culture? Herbert Schiller's answer was affirmative.[42] He contended that cultural domination is far from over but instead has become more pronounced. Coca-Colonization and McDonaldization of the world are emblematic of cultural imperialism. "In the contemporary world," James Petras also argued, "Hollywood, CNN and Disneyland are more influential than the Vatican, the Bible or the public relations rhetoric of political figures."[43]

Criticism of the presence of multinational advertising in the developing world is an extension of the media/cultural imperialism discourse. Herbert Schiller called the internationalization of advertising an act of "Madison Avenue imperialism," and Michael Anderson simply termed it "advertising imperialism."[44] Studies of the experiences of multinational ad agencies in the Third World, such as South and Southeast Asia and Latin America, have centered on the transformative impact of multinational advertising in the local cultural milieu.[45] The advertising imperialism discourse encompasses mainly three dimensions of cultural impact brought by multinational advertising in the Third World: 1) export of Western advertising and its professionalism; 2) transnationalization of consumer culture; and 3) commercialization of local mass media.[46]

However, to its critics, the media/cultural imperialism argument tacitly assumes the power and control of foreign cultural production in a local Third World setting on the one hand, and the uniformity of local audience reception on the other. As a corollary, the underlying assumptions of advertising imperialism appear also to be that ownership means control of advertising practice and content and that advertising messages are uniformly appreciated. Furthermore, the imperialism perspective seems to assume that there is a pure local/indigenous culture out there that is not only antithetical to Western values and norms but invariably vulnerable to foreign cultural "contamination" and domination as well. Charles F. Frazer challenged the idea of advertising imperialism. He was doubtful of the existence of the "great power" ascribed to Western advertising in the Third World and questioned the assumption that advertising effects are "unique and separable from those of other social forces" in the process of social and cultural change. When discussing whether advertising creates a consumer society, Frazer cited studies which showed that advertising only "changes the composition of consumption, not the level of consumption," and that advertising is the result (rather than the cause) of rise in income and consumption. He also challenged the assertion of the vulnerability of local cultures and the alleged culturally destructive nature of advertising.[47]

The imperialism discourse has demonstrated the critical vigilance in the face of the growing cultural circulation in the ever-expanding media world. But the term "media/cultural imperialism" still means just about anything anyone wants it to. Its adequacy as an analytical and explanatory tool has become suspect.

For both academic scholars and social commentators, cultural imperialism is interpreted as a process of imposed cultural homogenization. But the dynamics of cultural contact seem to defy such a linear and transparent explanation. The cultural convergence represented by the imperialism perspective slights the heterogenizing forces of local cultures. As Frederick Buell pointed out, ". . . [I]t seems increasingly intellectually retrograde and naive to evoke the specter of homogenization as the starting point for investigations of global cultural relationships."[48] Jan Nederveen Pieterse concurred that viewing globalization only in terms of homogenization was "empirically narrow and historically flat."[49] Lawrence W. Levine also argued that we should "stop talking about *dominance* and *purity* and begin thinking about *transformation*."[50]

Cultural change is historically the dialectical moment of homogenization and heterogenization. Such dynamics are perhaps as old as human society, though the (re)discovery and the debate of the theoretical conceptualization may be relatively recent. Socio-cultural transformation is always characterized by the concomitant movements of centripetal and centrifugal forces. Perhaps what is unique in the late 20th century is that with the aid of advanced communications technology, the scope and speed of social and cultural change is unprecedented in human history, and the role of the media and communication is ever more prominent and vital.

The concept of *glocalization* (a composite of "globalization" and "localization") takes into account both the global in the local and the local in the global.[51] "Ethnic and cultural fragmentation and modernist homogenization," Jonathan Friedman wrote, "are not two arguments, two opposing views of what is happening in the world today, but two constitutive trends of global reality."[52] The term "globalization" in much of the academic and popular press tends to imply only homogenization and uniformity. The imagery conjured up from Marshall McLuhan's "global village" metaphor is that of "coming together." Since the term "globalization" appeared to be occupied by the narrower notion of homogenization rather than the broader "the compression of the world," Roland Robertson felt it necessary to bring in "glocalization" to underscore that the global and the local are part and parcel in one process of social change. "The global is not in and of itself counterpoised to the local," Robertson pointed out, "rather, what is often referred to as the local is essentially included within the global." He further contended that "in this respect globalization . . . involves the linking of localities. But it also involves the 'invention' of locality. . . ."[53] Mike Featherstone echoed such analysis:[54] "What does seem clear is that it is not helpful to regard the global and local as dichotomies separated in space or time; rather, it would seem that the processes of globalization and localization are inextricably bound together in the current phase."

The outcome of globalization, as Anthony Giddens pointed out, "is not necessarily, or even usually, a generalized set of changes acting in a uniform direction, but consists in mutually opposed tendencies."[55] The inter-penetration and complementation between the local and the global thus yield a hybrid culture. The term "hybrid" came into popular use in the 19th century. Then it mainly referred to a physiological phenomenon (e.g., hybrid species); in the 20th century its meaning has been extended to the cultural realm.[56] Cultural hybridity "takes difference into sameness, and sameness into difference, but in a way that makes the same no longer the same, the different no longer simply different."[57] Ithiel de Sola Pool's contention that "foreign idea is appropriated as soon as it is imported" may sound a little too optimistic for every society, but his point about the indigenization process in cultural formations is illuminating.[58] When absorbing foreign media technology and content, traditional cultural values and visions can also be sustained by being "re-embedded" and "re-moored" in the new context. The notion of "re-embedding," in Giddens's view, complements that of "disembedding." By re-embedding, Giddens means "the reappropriation or recasting of disembedded social relations so as to pin them down (however partially or transitorily) to local conditions of time and place."[59] John B. Thompson also maintained that, instead of being abandoned, traditions can be taken up, "reshaped, transformed, perhaps even strengthened and reinvigorated through encountering with other ways of life."[60] It is therefore difficult to conceive that exposure of the local/indigenous culture to Western cultural products always taints the former. As Edward Said wrote,[61]

> Contamination is the wrong word to use here, but some notion of literature and indeed culture as hybrid (in Homi Bhaba's complex sense of that word) and encumbered, or

> entangled and overlapping with what used to be regarded as extraneous elements—this strikes me as the essential idea for the revolutionary realities today. . . .

In her study of occidentalism in the Chinese intellectual culture, Chen Xiaomei also observed, "Failure to recognize this indigenous use of Western discourses and the great variety of conditions that might provide the focus for its utterance can lead to fundamental problems in cross-cultural studies."[62]

In short, the local is not frozen spatially and temporally, awaiting the annihilation by the foreign. Nor do cultural encounters necessarily enervate the soul of the local and the indigenous. The presumed cultural purity and stability is only imaginary because culture evolves.

It is, however, also presumptuous for us to suggest that the interaction between globalization and localization always takes place on an equal level. It is henceforth useful to borrow the idea of a "continuum of hybridities" to make sense of the complexity and ambiguity of the global-local adaptation process. Jan Nederveen Pieterse defined the "continuum of hybridities"[63] as

> . . . on one end, an assimilationist hybridity that leans over towards the centre, adopts the canon and mimics the hegemony, and, at the other end, a destablizing hybridity that blurs the canon, reverses the current, subverts the centre. Hybridities, then, may be differentiated according to the components in the melange.

In short, contemporary cultural formation and change represents an interlocking duality of globalization and localization. As Arjun Appadurai stated, "The central problem of today's global interactions is the tension between cultural homogenization and cultural heterogenization."[64] If globalization is the defining thesis of contemporary society and culture and localization the antithesis, what remains to be uncovered is their synthesis. The research task thus becomes, according to Roland Robertson, "that of spelling out the ways in which homogenizing and heterogenization tendencies are mutually implicative. This is in fact more of an empirical problem than might at first be thought."[65]

This study of foreign advertising in China is a modest attempt to explore and explain the shifting dynamics between globalization and localization in the construction, communication, and consumption of advertising messages. It is a study of the role of foreign advertising in the Chinese advertising industry as well as in the Chinese consumers' "cultural imaginary." It aims to extend our understanding of the production and consumption of cultural artifacts, such as advertisements, in the increasingly globalized economic and media environment.

Scope and Structure of the Study

This book is structured into five parts to help shape a more comprehensive picture of the field of foreign advertising in China. The explanatory and interpretive strategy in this study considers not only the communicative representations in foreign ads but also the conditions of their production. To understand the activities of multinational ad agencies in contemporary China, it is first necessary to look at the historical development of the foreign advertising industry in that country. Foreign advertising is not a new phenomenon in China. It has a history. Advertising in China dates back to the early part of the 20th century. The 1920s and 1930s witnessed China's first advertising boom. During the first decades of the People's Republic, its development came to a halt as the country embarked on the road towards a centrally planned economy. Commercial advertising only returned in the late 1970s when China launched the market-oriented economic reform and reopened its economic and cultural doors to the West. Chapter 2 provides an overview of the history of foreign advertising in China, in relation to the Chinese economy and the mass media, from the early part of the 20th century to the 1990s.

Commercial advertising has become a fixture in the cityscape in China. Foreign advertising plays its part in reflecting as well as shaping the Chinese "cultural imaginary." Chapter 3 analyzes the form and content of foreign ads in the contemporary advertising environment. We try to uncover the "structure of attention" in the foreign ads and explore the ideals and values associated with the advertised goods. The description of the advertising content is supplemented by a discussion of a case of how a Chinese consumer may receive and interpret foreign ads.

The primary players in the advertising business include advertisers, advertising media, and advertising agencies; but it is the advertising agency that is "the spearhead of the advertising business."[66] What happens to a foreign ad agency when it enters a developing market such as China and begins to represent global consumer product manufacturers in a radically new setting? The ad agency becomes another site where the foreign meets the local. How is a foreign ad agency structurally organized in China? What is its workforce like? What is its culture of work? How is advertising professionalism defined? Chapter 4 focuses on a global advertising affiliate in Beijing. Based on participant observation and interviews, it is a behind-the-scenes look that attempts to bring to the fore the structural conditions in the making of advertising at this agency.

Another important player in the multinational advertising industry in China is the Chinese government. How has the Chinese regulatory regime affected foreign advertising content and practice? Chapter 5 explores the relationship between the Chinese government and the multinational advertising industry in China by examining the nature, process, and effectiveness of the governance of (foreign) advertising regulation. As one of the few nation-states still under a "communist" government as well as the world's largest potential consumer market, China presents an intriguing case for us to study the current tension between the nation-state and the global market.

Finally, in light of the theoretical debate between the imperialism perspective and the globalization thesis, Chapter 6 is devoted to a discussion of how the roles of the global and the local (or the foreign and the domestic) are negotiated in the case of foreign advertising in China. It is to be argued that in both the artifact and organization of foreign advertising in China, the global and local tendencies are intertwined in what Robert Young has called an "intricate process of cultural contact, intrusion, fusion and disjunction,"[67] constantly producing and reproducing a localized global and a globalized local. The role of foreign advertising in the development of Chinese advertising and consumer culture is also examined and assessed in this chapter.

2

The Advertising Revolution: Foreign Advertising in China in the 20th Century

Commercial advertising as a form of modern industry is a Western (and primarily American) invention. Its development has coincided with the emergence and growth of a capitalist consumer economy and the mass media. Advertising in its broadest sense (i.e., defined as making a product or service public and known) is perhaps as old as commercial activity. It was manifested in shop signs, store banners, product displays, and the hawking of street vendors to spread the message about the goods. There was nothing intrinsically Western or foreign about this type of advertising. It was and has been an integral part of Chinese commerce throughout history.

But modern advertising as an organized industry and "an institutionalized system of commercial information and persuasion"[1] that depends on the mass media, emerged as an emblem of

American society and culture in the late 19th and early 20th centuries.[2] Its development was intimately bound with the rise of a consumer economy.[3] The level of advertising and marketing is commensurate with the stage of development in a market-oriented economy. Modern advertising also depends on the availability of the mass media to serve as channels and vehicles. The symbiosis among economy, media, and advertising compels us to cast the discussion of the history of foreign advertising in China within the context of Chinese economy and media.

The presence of a foreign advertising industry in China is no historic accident. It has been formed by the economic forces both inside and outside the Chinese society and the development of China's mass media system. The best starting point is China's trade with foreign colonial powers at the turn of the century.

The Rise of Foreign Advertising: The Pre-1949 Years

Western countries approached China via the medium of trade.[4] China's trade with the West can be traced back at least to the 17th century, but it only became full-fledged in the aftermath of the Sino-British Opium War in the mid-19th century. The direction of trade between China and the West had then shifted from China selling more to buying more from foreign countries.

The impact of the changing pattern of flow of goods and capital was profound for the Chinese society. Before the opening of major Chinese ports to Western colonial powers, the riches of China, material or imaginary, and Chinese civilization in general had played a greater part in Western life than the West did in China.[5] With its worldwide ascendance since the 18th and 19th centuries, Western civilization has not only reached China's shores but also has engendered a revolution in the consciousness as well as the material being of the Chinese people.

In the 30 years between 1864 and 1894, China's trade with foreign countries grew more than twofold, with more imports than exports, and the imports were mostly consumer products.[6] Between 1912 and 1928, China's foreign trade, though expanded in general, consistently showed a deficit.[7] Foreign investment in

Table 2.1 Foreign investment in China as a percentage by country, 1902–1936

Country	1902	1914	1931	1936
Great Britain	33.0	37.7	36.7	35.0
Japan	0.1	13.6	35.1	40.0
Russia	31.1	16.7	8.4	0.0
United States	2.5	3.1	6.1	8.6
France	11.6	10.7	5.9	6.7
Germany	20.9	16.4	2.7	4.3
Belgium	0.6	1.4	2.7	1.7
Netherlands	0.0	0.0	0.9	0.0
Italy	0.0	0.0	1.4	2.1
Scandinavia	0.0	0.0	0.1	0.0
Others	0.0	0.4	0.0	1.6
TOTAL (US millions)	$787.9	$1610.3	$3242.5	$3483.2

Adapted from Chi-ming Hou, *Foreign Investment and Economic Development in China, 1840-1937,* p. 17. Cambridge: Harvard University Press, 1965.

China grew from US$787.9 million in 1902 to nearly US$3.5 billion in 1936 (Table 2.1).

Towards the end of the 19th century, about 200 foreign-owned factories had been set up in the country.[8] By 1907, for example, foreign capital had dominated China's shipping, railway, and iron-ore production businesses; and almost one-third of cotton yarn spinning was under the control of foreign capital.[9] Foreign imports and foreign production of cotton inside China had then garnered most of the market share.[10] In 1918, there were already 7,000 offices and branches of foreign companies in China, representing a wide range of industries and services.[11]

At the dawn of the 20th century, Britain, Russia, and Germany were the three leading creditors of foreign direct investment in China. A decade or so later, Britain took a commanding lead, distantly followed by Russia, Germany, and Japan. During the 1930s, Japan's economic interest and influence rose. In 1931 Britain and Japan were the two largest investors in China. About the time of the Sino-Japanese War, Japan became the largest creditor country.

After the Sino-British Opium War of the mid-19th century, foreign trade and investment attained tremendous growth in the Chinese economy. As a result of the economic and military expansion of Western powers into China, the self-proclaimed "central kingdom" finally lost its closed state of mind and being. China was thrust into an international (economic) system and, in the meantime, its mentality of being the center of the world drastically shifted to that of being on the periphery.

Westerners not only brought in goods and capital but also introduced China to modern mass media. The first modern newspapers in China were established by Western missionaries in the trading ports in the 19th century. These newspapers were fundamentally a means of spreading the gospel of Christianity, but also reported news and introduced modern science and technology. During this period, *Chinese Serial,* a monthly founded in Hong Kong in 1853, noted in an article in its December 1854 issue that the paper would begin to carry advertising starting with its next issue. The article said, "If China can emulate that (advertising practice in the Western countries), it would be of great benefit." Due to its format and size, the *Chinese Serial* would not print ads amidst the articles but would attach them at the end.[12]

The first two major Chinese-language newspapers were spin-offs of foreign language publications. The *Chinese and Foreign Gazette* was established in 1858, and three years later *Shanghai News* went into publication. Both papers carried commercial advertising.[13] During the first half of the 20th century, the *Shun Pao* and *Sin Wan Pao,* based in Shanghai, were the two most influential Chinese-language daily newspapers. Originally founded by foreign companies, they later became Chinese owned and both papers were partly financed by advertising.[14] The *Shun Pao* carried advertising in its 1872 inaugural issue and, according to one study, almost 60% of its space in 1925 was devoted to advertising, more than half of which was commercial advertising.[15] The paper claimed in its own promotional advertising in 1936 that "an advertisement in the *Shun Pao* is read by at least 150,000 families, in all parts of China."[16]

Foreign-language newspapers, mainly serving expatriates in

China, were also important advertising vehicles. The most prominent ones in Shanghai were *North China Daily News, Shanghai Mercury, Shanghai Press, Shanghai Times, Le Journal de Shanghai, Der Ostasiatischer Lloyd, The Shanghai Zaria,* and *The Shanghai Mainichi Shimbun.*[17] The *North China Daily News,* according to its ad, had an average daily circulation of 10,350 copies for the month of June 1936 and was "the only newspaper in the Far East which publishes periodical audited net circulation statements."[18] The *Le Journal de Shanghai* claimed that it is "the ONLY French newspaper in Shanghai. The ONLY newspaper entirely devoted to French interests. The ONLY newspaper which is read by ALL French residents in this city. . . . Its advertising pages offer the quickest and cheapest way of reaching the French buying public."[19] Established in 1925, *The Shanghai Zaria* advertised itself as the oldest Russian newspaper in Shanghai.[20] Advertisers were attracted to foreign-language newspapers because it was generally cheaper to advertise in them, and they usually offered a higher commission rate to agencies than the major Chinese-language newspapers.[21] Perhaps, more important, as the ad for the *Shanghai Times* and the *Shanghai Sunday Times* stated, these newspapers had "an international appeal" and were read by the "real purchasing classes, Chinese and Foreign."[22] By 1936, with a population of about 3,500,000, Shanghai (the world's sixth largest city) was China's most cosmopolitan city and boasted 36 newspapers with a combined daily circulation of almost 900,000.[23]

Magazines and periodicals also began to flourish during the 1920s and 1930s. There were nearly 2,000 periodicals reaching a reading audience of over 30 million people in China.[24] The most notable titles in Shanghai, for instance, included the *Eastern Miscellany, Saturday, Happy Home,* and *Young Companion. Happy Home* and *Women's Pictorial* catered primarily to a female readership and carried much advertising.[25] *Shopping News* claimed that it was "read and believed in by women in China" and had an audited weekly circulation of 6,200 copies. The magazine advertised itself as "the only publication in China whose advertising policy is based upon that of *Good Housekeeping* magazine" and that it was "the only publication in China which keeps abreast of Fashions, Food and Feminine News. . . ."[26] The *Young Companion,* a pictorial magazine with a circulation of 40,000 copies in 1936, promoted itself as "the most attractive and popular magazine in China."[27] A 1931 study of one of China's most popular magazines showed that after it went from a monthly to a biweekly in 1919 its advertising content, previously less than 500 pages annually, increased to about 800 in 1920.[28] In short, these consumer-oriented magazines had become viable vehicles for commercial advertising.

Another advertising vehicle, radio, was introduced by the American journalist E.G. Osborn in Shanghai in 1923. By the mid-1930s, radio stations, commercial as well as state-owned, had sprung up in most of China's major cities. Aside from entertainment and news they also broadcast advertising spots. A travel book on Shanghai published in 1934 listed the city's foreign radio stations, such as Radio Shanghai and China Broadcast. The book also stated that "ninety per cent of all radio sets in Shanghai go to Chinese and a large portion of radio advertising is placed with the Chinese broadcasting stations."[29] Local advertisers did use radio to advertise and the results appeared to be satisfactory.[30] By 1937, there were 78 broadcast stations nationwide and 20,000 radio receivers in China.[31]

The presence and activities of Western merchants and missionaries played a pivotal role in the emergence of modern mass media in China at the turn of the century. By the 1930s this media evolution had reached a high point.[32] But its development was extremely uneven, with most of it concentrated in a few port cities, especially Shanghai.[33] Advertising thus developed naturally along the flow of goods into China; it was employed principally to promote these goods and expand sales in the untapped Chinese market. As Baiyi Xu noted,[34]

> In the late 19th and early 20th centuries, most foreign goods gained acceptance through constant advertising in the modern media. These novel vehicles for advertising—mass publications from modern presses, radio broadcast-

ing, electronic displays—arrived in China along with the foreign commodities.

It was the foreign companies that first advertised in newspapers, magazines, and on billboards in China. Most of the early newspaper ads were for foreign products. Because of a high illiteracy rate among the Chinese population, billboards turned out to be one of the most effective advertising mediums. The majority of these were conceived and erected by foreign advertisers and agencies.[35] In 1915 an Italian named Bruno Perme established the first foreign ad agency in Shanghai, and its business was primarily outdoor billboards.[36] During the 1920s and 1930s Carl Crow, Inc., Millington's Advertising Co., Consolidated National Advertising Corporation, and China Commercial Advertising Agency became known as the Big Four in China's burgeoning advertising industry (Table 2.2). They were all based in Shanghai. Ideally located at China's commercial center, these four agencies most likely were the largest agencies in the country at that time. A few smaller agencies were based in other cities, such as Beijing, Tianjin, Chongqing and Guangzhou. According to one account, there were about 30 advertising agencies in Shanghai in 1937, of which five were foreign owned.[37] Carl Crow, Inc. and Millington's

Table 2.2 Four major ad agencies in Shanghai during the 1920s and 1930s

Agency	Year established	Founder	Foreign connection
Carl Crow, Inc.	1918	Carl Crow	American journalist
Millington's Advertising Co.	1921	F.C. Millington	Englishman
China Commercial Advertising Agency	1926	C.P. Ling	Educated in the U.S.
Consolidated National Advertising Co.	1930	T.B. Chang	Agency manager with U.S. education

Advertising Co. were among these foreign agencies. Also included was the advertising department of the French-owned Oriental Press, which was quite active at the time.[38]

Carl Crow, Inc. was one of the pioneering agencies in China. Carl Crow (1883–1945), a native of Missouri, was the founder and proprietor of one of the most successful ad agencies in Shanghai during the 1920s and 1930s. Arriving in China as a journalist in 1911, he was employed as an associate city editor for the *China Press,* the first American newspaper in Shanghai. He stayed at the paper for 18 months before departing for New York City. In 1916 Crow returned to China as the Far East representative of the U.S. Committee on Public Information. As a child he had developed a strong interest in advertising, Crow wrote, and in 1918 he started his own advertising business in Shanghai. His best-seller, *Four Hundred Million Customers* (1937), which won an award from the American Booksellers Association and was translated into several foreign languages, recounted interesting tales of his advertising adventure in China.[39]

Over a span of 20 years, Crow ran a successful advertising operation, and his advertising company was credited with teaching the Chinese new consumption behavior. Back in the early 1920s, Crow's agency placed lipstick and vanishing cream ads in Chinese newspapers.

> Thanks to our efforts and the liberal advertising appropriations of our clients, a good many Chinese girls have been taught to put on vanishing cream as a base for powder and rouge and the use of cold cream at night, rubbing it into the pores of the skin.[40]

Through advertising, Crow also helped engender a sartorial revolution for Chinese women—from trousers to skirts. He proudly proclaimed that "we brought out the first one (fashion book) and that we played our small part in revealing the most beautiful leg the world has ever seen."[41] For the Chinese women the new styles of clothing were loud and clear statements of modernity, an idea the country began to embrace.

Crow's advertising also contributed to the introduction of raisins, which were previously unknown in China.[42] In spite of his successes Crow admitted that reorienting Chinese consumers' eating habits was not an easy matter and, furthermore, was not always possible. He did not believe, for instance, that any amount of advertising could ever substantially change the Chinese diet.[43] He observed that although foreigners brought milk, butter, and cheese to the attention of Chinese consumers, these dairy products were not widely accepted into the Chinese diet. Similarly, the tendency for Chinese to choose traditional Chinese medicine as a cure for their illnesses also presented obstacles for the promotion of Western pharmaceutical products. This, however, did not discourage foreign manufacturers from advertising patent medicines in China; in fact, newspapers in those days were full of medical advertising.[44]

An ad for Carl Crow, Inc., titled "The Wasted Half Dollar," appeared in the company's 1937 edition of the *Newspaper Directory of China*:[45]

> John Wannamaker, whose fortune was founded on successful advertising, once said that he felt sure that one-half of every dollar he had ever spent for advertising had been wasted, but he was never sure which half of the dollar it was. The problem of the wasted half dollar in advertising expenditure is one which will never be solved, because advertising is an intangible force which can not be measured by a foot rule or checked on a cash register. The fact that with such an admitted wastage advertising remains such a potent and growing factor in business proves its efficacy.
>
> We can, in many ways, help you to save at least a part of that wasted half dollar. For example, we have been placing and checking the results from advertising in a great many publications in China for more than a decade. We know, for example, not by one test but by hundreds, that certain publications can be counted on to secure certain results. We also know that other publications which receive a great amount of the advertisers' money are practically valueless.

> We would be glad to discuss your next advertising plans with you and without any obligation on your part. Suppose you write us today: Carl Crow, Inc., 81 Jinkee Road, Shanghai.

Unlike today's global advertising network, Carl Crow, Inc. was independently owned. When the Sino-Japanese War broke out in 1937, Crow retreated from China and subsequently did not return.[46]

Two of the agencies in the Big Four during the 1920s and 1930s were Chinese companies. Both C.P. Ling, founder of the China Commercial Advertising Agency, and L. Lewis Mason, manager of the Consolidated National Advertising Co., had earlier studied in the United States. Ling received his B.A. degree from Rochester University and went on to obtain an M.A. degree from Columbia University. He studied advertising at Columbia and started his ad agency in Shanghai in 1926. When it celebrated its 10th anniversary in 1936, China Commercial Advertising Agency claimed to have a roster of 97 clients, including Heinz, Parker Pen, Gillette Industries, Quaker Oats, and Welch Grape Juice.[47] Xu Baiyi, a copywriter at the Consolidated National Advertising Co., received advertising training through a correspondence course from the Dixon School of Advertising in London.[48] These advertising professionals, by way of learning the trade from Western practices, became the pioneers in modern Chinese advertising.

Not surprisingly, advertising then concentrated on and appeared most effective in the marketing of such consumer goods as cosmetics, fashion, food, and pharmaceuticals. Patent medicine and cigarette manufacturers were initially the two major advertisers. Among commercial ads in the *Shun Pao* in 1925, those featuring medicine appeared most frequently.[49] Consumer advertising predominantly targeted the affluent Chinese, a small segment of the population, and Western expatriates in the foreign enclaves in the Chinese cities. As the *Shun Pao* ad said, "The *Shun Pao* is the best medium for foreign advertising as only people of high purchasing power, like the readers of the *Shun Pao*, buy high-class imported goods."[50]

But mass marketing and advertising was still possible. By introducing the Mei Foo lamp (a kerosene lamp), the Standard Oil Company was the first to succeed in mass merchandising a foreign product in China.[51] Like scotch and gin that were exotic drinks to Chinese consumers, cigarettes were then still a novelty in China where water-pipe (a variation of smoking) had been the tradition. But it did not take long before foreign brands dominated the Chinese cigarette market. The British-American Tobacco Company (BAT) was the biggest player. "The BAT advertising system," wrote Sherman Cochran, "left no region of China untouched." BAT's advertising campaigns were so extensive and effective that one Chinese journalist remarked that "many rural Chinese villages still don't know who in the world Sun Yat-sen (a prominent Chinese leader) is, but very few places have not known Ruby Queen (a BAT brand) [of] cigarettes."[52] In 1928, the largest neon sign, erected in one of the busiest sections of Shanghai, advertised a BAT brand.[53]

To accurately represent the ideals and aesthetics of Chinese consumers, foreign advertisers and ad agencies hired local Chinese graphic artists to design their advertisements. At first BAT hired Westerners, but the German fairy-tales and the advertising slogans they used hardly made any sense to the local Chinese. BAT then decided to commission Chinese artists and writers, who drew from the wellspring of Chinese folklore and popular culture, and BAT's advertising became successfully adapted to the Chinese cultural setting.[54]

Introducing foreign goods to China was nevertheless not always an easy task. Foreign goods were often clearly identified with the word *yang* (literally means "foreign") added to the name of the item.[55] Imported goods were thus easily differentiated from local brands. A related factor, probably of more significance, was that it was simply difficult to persuade people to break away from their existing consumption habits and accept new foreign products. In addition, periodic nationalistic boycotts during the early part of the century compounded the difficulty to advertise and promote foreign products in China. In 1915, for instance, BAT suffered badly from the nationalistic advertising campaigns by the local Nanyang Tobacco Company in the midst of the "national goods movement;" on the other hand, BAT, as an American-British company, benefited from an anti-Japanese boycott in 1919.[56]

It was only after the opening of Chinese ports to foreign economies and the Chinese market to foreign products that Chinese people came to know about the practice of commercial advertising, from its role and function to its form and content. China's first major encounter with foreign consumer products and culture through the medium of advertising during the 1920s and 1930s seemed to have left a deep imprint on Chinese economic and cultural life. As Xu Baiyi recounted,

> The Chinese began wearing clothes made from imported fabrics and sewn on Singer machines. Bread was introduced, becoming more and more popular as an alternative to the traditional rice, steamed bun, and porridge. Milk became a daily drink of the upper class. The number of brands of coffee on the market, including Maxwell House, Del Monte, and Hills Brothers, attested to the fact that the Chinese were becoming coffee drinkers. The introduction of concrete changed Chinese construction practices forever. Instead of salt, the Chinese began using toothpaste to brush their teeth. Patent medicines provided an alternative to medicinal herbs. Street cars and bay carts joined the ricksha on China's teeming city streets.[57]

Advertising's role and influence in China was altered dramatically when the Chinese Communist Party came into power in 1949. The subsequent changes in its overall development strategies and policies diminished the role of commercial advertising and eventually eliminated advertising as a necessary marketing tool.

The Fall into Oblivion: The First Decades of the PRC

After 1949 the People's Republic of China (PRC) embarked on a different road to development and modernization. The Chinese government under Mao Zedong implemented a highly centralized economic, political, and cultural structure. Private ownership and production were abolished through consolidation with government-owned enterprises in the urban areas and through the commune system in the rural countryside. The central government exercised firm control over economic planning and implementation. Little local autonomy was allowed. The restructuring of the Chinese economy during the first decades of the PRC was also exemplified by the development priority of heavy industry over the service sector. Consumption was discouraged, and many of the food staples and other daily necessities became rationed.

In addition, China allied with and drew support from the Soviet-led socialist camp in the 1950s. It later adopted a policy of self-reliance. For three decades, China's economic contacts with Western industrialized economies had been extremely limited. The dominant ideology then was that China should rely on the "wisdom of the masses" to seek economic development rather than attracting foreign investment and pursuing international trade.[58] Long after the founding of the People's Republic, imports and trade in general remained relatively stationary. A dramatic increase occurred only in the second half of the 1970s when the Chinese government began to reopen its doors and encouraged investment from the West.

In short, three main developments characterized the economic structure in the first decades of the PRC: the institutionalization of a centrally planned economy, the development emphasis on heavy industry, and the limited role of trading with Western economies. The primary economic problem facing China was understood as the production rather than the distribution and consumption of goods. These developments hindered the growth of the advertising industry. Eventually, with the changing function of the media, they rendered commercial advertising irrelevant in the country's socialist economy.

The centralized social structure under Mao Zedong's government also placed constraints on the Chinese mass media. Media outlets were limited, and the media system was extremely centralized. Especially during the Cultural Revolution (1966-1976), there was a drastic decline in the number of newspapers and magazines. In 1965, for instance, there were 343 newspapers and 790 magazine titles in publication; but the numbers dropped to 42 and 21 respectively in 1970. The broadcast media seemed less affected by the turmoil during the heyday of the Cultural Revolution (1966-1968), and television had just started to develop.[59]

Media outlets during the first decades of the PRC did not become vehicles for advertising. Two fundamental changes in the function and structure of the Chinese media had in principle as well as in practice inhibited the growth of advertising. First, the chief function of the media had become the propagation of communist ideology. Information dissemination (including economic information) had to support party lines and government policies. Second, state ownership of mass media decreased the role of advertising in media financing and management. The government also subsidized newspaper and magazine subscriptions. In a word, the nature of the Chinese media had turned from partially commercial during the pre-PRC years to totally political.

Advertising continued to be part of the economic life in China during the Sino-Japanese War (1937-1945) and the Civil War (1945-1949). At the dawn of the Communist victory in China's Civil War, there were about 90 ad agencies in Shanghai.[60] In 1950, the ad agency association in Shanghai had a registered membership of about 100.[61] The Chinese government started to transform private ownership into state ownership, and declared the completion of the reformation of private businesses by 1956. In Shanghai, 108 ad agencies were consolidated into one state entity called the Shanghai Advertising Corporation.[62]

With the transformation in China's economic structure and mass media, advertising became increasingly irrelevant as a viable marketing tool. The advertising income of the *People's Daily* (the flagship publication of the Chinese government) between 1950 and 1970 showed a sharp decrease from the period of 1956-1960 (6,531,000 yuan) to 1961-1966 (734,000 yuan) and 1967-1970 (189,000 yuan).[63] However, the communication potential of advertising had not been ignored. In 1957, the Chinese government sent a delegation from its Ministry of Commerce to attend the

Prague Conference of Advertising Workers of Socialist Countries. At a meeting on commercial advertising in Shanghai two years later, the Chinese government outlined the concept of socialist advertising. Socialist advertising must serve the purposes of production, consumption, distribution, and beautification of the urban environment, and must not only be true and artistic but also reflect policy, ideology, and cultural identity.[64] Instead of serving commercial interests, advertising began to be seen as a communication tool to showcase China's economic achievement. Advertising had, in other words, become political marketing rather than the conventional promotion of goods and services. As James Chu observed, "Advertising in China is a form of political propaganda. It advertises the success of the economic policy and the progress toward modernization."[65]

Outdoor advertising became the first casualty when the Cultural Revolution began. Commercial messages on billboards were replaced with political propaganda; neon signs for shops and products were destroyed. The Shanghai Advertising Corporation was renamed the Shanghai Fine Arts Company, whose main duty was to design political propaganda posters. Countless goods became "problem products" overnight. The likes of cosmetics, jewelry, Western-style dress, traditional Chinese dishes, chocolate, and whiskey were thought as embodying feudal and bourgeois lifestyles, which countered against the prevailing proletarian ideology; brand names, logos, and advertisements that evoked traditional cultural motifs and themes were also regarded as problematic. Many brands and stores adopted new names, such as "Red Guard," "People," and "Workers and Peasants."[66] Although the *People's Daily* ran industrial ads until 1970,[67] commercial advertising, deemed as a wasteful capitalist business practice, could not possibly survive in the drastically changed political, economic climate and media environment. It eventually fell into oblivion.

On arriving in Guangzhou for the Canton Trade Fair in the mid-1960s, a French promotion specialist kept wondering why the city appeared so drab and dull to him. It suddenly dawned on him that the bleakness was because of the total absence of advertising: "The colorful posters, the brilliant neon signs which brighten the capitalistic cities were entirely lacking."[68]

The Return of Advertising: The Reform Era

China's open-door policy in the late 1970s was welcomed by the world's developed economies. Redirecting the policy priority to economic development, the Third Plenary Session of the 11th Congress of the Chinese Communist Party in 1978 was heralded as another watershed in Chinese national politics. Since the implementation of the economic reform policies, there has been a phenomenal increase in the influx of foreign goods and capital into China. One concomitant development of the expansion of foreign business was the return of foreign advertising in the Chinese market.

A central rule of market economy appears to be that the saturation of the home market leads a company to expand to overseas markets in order to realize continuing profit. The convergence of political, economic, and technological forces since the 1980s has facilitated the boom in international business. Multinational corporations are becoming powerful institutions that link production and consumption around the world.

The expansion of multinational companies is generally made possible through capital investment, a major form of which is foreign direct investment (FDI). FDI grew rapidly worldwide in the 1980s and continued to flourish in the 1990s. The global volume of FDI reached almost US$2 trillion in 1992, generating about US$5.5 trillion in sales around the world.[69] The United States, Great Britain, Japan, Germany, and France led the nations of the world in having the most outflow of FDI. In the 1980s the flow of FDI was concentrated within the Triad (i.e., the European Community, Japan, and the United States). In the 1990s the inflow of FDI into developed countries started to decline, but that to less-developed countries increased, especially to Asia and Latin America. By the early 1990s there were 37,000 multinational corporations in the world, with more than 170,000 foreign affiliates. More than 91% of their parent companies were based in developed countries, but only about half of the 170,000 foreign affiliates were in developed countries.[70]

Companies, large and small, are now more likely than at any other time in history to venture into foreign markets for growth. The 1996 *Business Week* Global 1000 Report indicates, "From the U.S. to Europe to Japan, the companies moving up the rankings are those that have become worldwide names in technology, manufacturing, and consumer goods."[71] For many businesses in the West, foreign earnings command increasing weight in their total income. Take the example of the U.S.-based Coca-Cola Company. Eighty percent of its profit came from its overseas market in 1993.[72] Another case in point is McDonald's, which had set up franchise stores in 53 countries by 1990, and the number of countries with golden arches increased to 94 in 1996.[73] McDonald's, Coca-Cola, Walt Disney, Kodak, Sony, Gillette, Mercedes Benz, Levi's, Microsoft, and Marlboro have become brand leaders around the world.[74]

The flow of goods and capital between countries includes and partly depends on the flow of information.[75] With the increasing integration of the world economy, the global spread of advertising seems inevitable. The history of the international expansion of the ad agency J. Walter Thompson is illustrative in this respect. The agency's internationalization "parallels more closely than any other the worldwide expansion of the great American enterprises. . . ."[76] For the large U.S. advertising agencies, their overseas income grew faster than their domestic income.[77] Much of the advertising growth has taken place in developing markets such as China and Mexico.

The changes of development strategies from Chinese leaders Mao Zedong to Deng Xiaoping have transformed China's economic and social structure. After reopening its doors to the West in the late 1970s, China was reintegrated into the capitalist world economy in a surprisingly short time. China's trading partners have quickly become diversified, crossing political and ideological divides. Enticed by a great potential consumer market and a cheap labor pool, multinational companies have been setting up operations on the Chinese mainland.

The influx of foreign goods and capital into China increased rapidly from 1978 to 1994. The value of imports grew from about US$10 billion in 1978 to over US$115 billion in 1994.[78] The increase in foreign investment was even more dramatic, from US$100 million between 1979 and 1980 to more than US$45 billion in 1994.[79] For three consecutive years since 1993, China was the largest recipient of foreign direct investment among the developing countries, and came in second overall, after the United States.[80] By March 1996, about 260,000 businesses with foreign investment had been registered in China, and the total amount of foreign investment soared to over US$140 billion.[81] Over 300 of the world's largest 500 multinational companies have by now invested in the Chinese market.[82] As Nicholas R. Lardy summarized,[83]

> In the almost two decades since economic reform began in China the role of the foreign sector has burgeoned in ways that no one anticipated. The volume of foreign trade and the role of foreign capital are both far greater than could have been foreseen based on the modest Chinese economic reforms initiated in the late 1970s. By the mid-1990s, China had become one of the world's largest trading nations, the recipient of more foreign direct investment than any other country in the world, the largest borrower from the World Bank, the largest recipient of official development assistance in the form of low-interest, long-term concessionary loans from industrialized countries, and, except for the Czech Republic, the only transition economy with ready access to international capital and equity markets.

Decentralization is another defining theme in the post-Mao economic restructuring. Provincial and regional governments have achieved greater autonomy in decision making. One manifestation of the decentralization effort, for example, is the changing budgetary relationship between the central and provincial governments.[84] The budgetary reform went back and forth between centralization and decentralization, but the overall direction of change was in favor of provincial governments, which can now retain more revenue for their own investment and development. The general policy of decentralization has also affected China's media structure and management.

"Amidst the domestic changes and global challenges of the 1980s and 1990s," wrote Judy Polumbaum,[85] "Chinese newspapers, magazines, radio, television, and other media have increased in number, expanded in scope and ambition, and become ever more variegated in character and content." Polumbaum's observation captured the astounding growth of the Chinese mass media in the reform era. Although it is difficult to gauge whether media development is a result of or a cause for advertising development, it is nevertheless indisputable that the expanded space and time in China's media environment furnished a necessary condition for the return and growth of advertising.

At the beginning of the 1980s when the reform policies were first implemented, there were fewer than 200 newspapers (published at or above the provincial level); but by the beginning of 1996 the number of newspapers in publication had reached an unprecedented total of 2,235 nationwide.[86] Not only did the number of newspapers grow dramatically, they also expanded with added pages, weekend editions, and even regional and overseas editions. With the newspaper expansion, more advertising space was made available.

Magazine publishing experienced similar growth. In the early 1980s, there were a little over 2,000 magazines in China. By the end of 1994, more than 8,000 titles were in publication.[87] Besides the sheer growth in numbers, it is also important to note that many of the new entries in the magazine and newspaper industry are purely entertainment/diversion oriented.

China did not experiment with television broadcasting until 1956. Television grew fastest in the 1980s and 1990s. In 1985, there were 202 television stations; and 10 years later the number surged to over 980. Television now reaches more than 87% of the Chinese population, and the television audience can sometimes be as large as 900 million.[88] With the proliferation of TV stations, TV programming has also been expanded with added time. Several stations have established 24-hour channels (e.g., CCTV Channel 4). In addition, cable television started to develop in China in the mid-1980s, and many cities are now wired for cable. According to one report, there were already more than 1,200 cable stations around the country in 1995.[89]

As a cost-effective way to disseminate information to the largely agrarian population, radio was accorded great significance during the first decades of the PRC. Its development continued during the reform era. The whole country had only 38 radio stations in 1980, but by the early 1990s the number of stations had risen to 586. In June 1995 there were 1,107 radio stations nationwide, reaching 77.5% of the population.[90] Another noteworthy development in radio is the creation of specialized stations. In 1992 Shanghai People's Radio mutated into eight separate stations—news, market information, traffic information, entertainment, music, foreign language education, English, and a variety station. Guangzhou Radio started to broadcast round-the-clock in 1991. These developments resulted in not only increased programming but also increased variety.

In addition, Chinese editions of Western magazines, such as *Elle, Business Week,* and *Forbes,* have been launched by multinational publishers in cooperation with mainland Chinese or Hong Kong publishers.[91] In 1994 the U.S. media giant Time-Warner reached an agreement with the Chinese government film agency to distribute 10 Hollywood blockbuster films in China every year. The restriction of 10 movies a year was dropped after the U.S.-China trade negotiations in June 1996.[92] Chinese versions of "Entertainment Tonight" and "Sesame Street" have become part of the Chinese TV menu. Although the Chinese government still forbids foreign companies from owning publications and programs in China, foreign media companies have achieved some success in negotiating their way into the Chinese market through joint agreements.

In sum, there has been a remarkable growth of media outlets and an increasing amount of air time and ad space to be filled in the Chinese media. Such media developments created a favorable environment for the reintroduction and growth of commercial advertising. Just as important (if not more so) to the relegitimization of advertising are the changes in the function and structure of the Chinese media. While the government does not officially relinquish media's propaganda role, it espouses a compromising policy of "managing public institutional units *via* the methods of managing business units."[93] For the major Chinese media, propaganda and profit are equally important; without one or the other they will be unable to survive. The government still subsidizes media operations in many ways even though the level of support is only partial.

Advertising has become a legitimate and, in most cases, an indispensable source of income for the Chinese media. There was an explosive growth of advertising spending in the four major media, particularly in newspaper and television. Commercialization of the Chinese media is well underway even amidst the repeated official declarations of media being in the service of the state. The Chinese media have ceased to be monolithic, and entertainment-oriented newspapers and magazines, totally devoid of political propaganda, have become lucrative businesses and flood the Chinese media market.

As an important part of China's drive toward a market economy, advertising reappeared in the Chinese mass media in January 1979. The Chinese government realized the crucial role of advertising in its market-oriented reform. In his speech at the Third World Advertising Congress held in Beijing in June 1987, Wan Li, then China's acting premier, maintained, "Advertising links production and consumption. It is an important part of the economic activities of modern society. It has become an indispensable element in the promotion of economic prosperity."[94] Zheng Heping, Director of the Advertising Bureau of the State Administration for Industry and Commerce, wrote that advertising had been mistakenly treated as a tool of political propaganda in China under the centralized command economy. He stated that advertising is primarily a market behavior and an instrument for economic competition.[95] It was often argued in the Chinese press that the function of advertising was as important in a socialist country as in a capitalist economy.[96]

Shanghai TV made history in January 1979 when it aired the first television commercial in China (a one-and-a-half-minute ad for a Chinese medicinal wine). The Shanghai-based *Liberation Daily* carried the first print ad (for Minolta camera) after an almost 10-year absence of advertising in the Chinese press. As of March 1979, there were three locations approved for billboard advertising in Shanghai.[97] The *People's Daily*, the authoritative voice of the Chinese government, started to publish commercial ads in April of that year.[98] It is important to note that all these efforts to restore advertising were initiatives endorsed by the propaganda ministry of the central government.[99]

In spite of such official support, the reintroduction of advertising was not a smooth process. The government faced the challenge of legitimizing something that it had earlier vehemently denounced. Attacks on advertising were particularly vocal during the anti-spiritual pollution campaign in 1983-1984. Domestic advertising was criticized for embracing the profit motive of Western advertising; some had reservations about placing ads for foreign businesses in prominent places.[100] As another element of the growing pains, during the anti-bourgeois-liberalization campaign in 1987, dozens of outdoor billboards were ordered to be removed.[101] Nonetheless, like the general economic reform policies, commercial advertising withstood all these criticisms and challenges, and continued to expand and prosper, especially in the 1990s.

Despite its near disappearance from the Chinese society as an outcome of the socialist command economy, commercial advertising has experienced rapid growth since China embarked on its market-oriented reform. In 1981, the gross advertising revenue made up about 0.02% of China's GNP (as compared to 0.95% in Japan around the same time).[102] In spite of the insignificant start, the Chinese advertising industry achieved an annual growth of about 48% between 1981 and 1995. Its percentage share in China's GNP rose remarkably to 0.47% in 1995. By the end of 1995, China's advertising revenue had reached 27.3 billion yuan (US$3.29 billion).[103] The number of advertising firms had grown from 1,169 in 1981 to 57,024 by 1997. There were fewer than

20,000 employees in the advertising industry in the early 1980s but the total increased to half a million in the mid-1990s.[104]

The sheer number of the advertising businesses may be huge, but the firms are generally small. Of the 48,082 advertising businesses registered in 1995, only about one-quarter of them were *bone fide* full-service advertising agencies. The rest only engaged in certain aspects of advertising (e.g., creative or media buying). Some are simply ghost agencies. There are, on the average, fewer than 10 people in each advertising shop. This figure has remained steady over the years.

The Chinese advertising industry is also characterized by an unbalanced agency-media relationship, with overpowering media and weak agencies. Despite the proliferation of media outlets and the decentralization of media management, media monopoly by the government still prevails and only in rare cases is there genuine competition. Wielding their tremendous social and political influence, media organizations often expand their reach into advertising by setting up their own shops to compete with ad agencies. They quote lower rates to court advertisers. The ad agency and the media often find themselves in head-on competition for clients.

For the Chinese advertisers, ad placement often takes precedence over ad production. Chinese advertisers and ad agencies put heavy emphasis on buying media time while ignoring ad execution and production quality. The most revealing example is the public bidding for 1996 prime time spots on China Central Television (CCTV) (12 five-second spots immediately after the 7 o'clock nightly news). Two Chinese distilled spirit producers won the bidding. The top bidder paid almost 13 million yuan (approximately US$1.6 million) per second for the five-second spot, which probably set the world record for the most expensive ad.[105] The fact that the company spent half of its annual revenue on TV advertising caused heated debate about whether it was a waste of money or a sound marketing decision. Chinese ads generally are created without sufficient product, market, and media analysis. To most Chinese advertisers, the notion of marketing and advertising is still tantamount to where to place the ad.

By and large, the economically more-developed coastal region represents the top echelon of advertising development, with the inland region in the middle, and the outlying areas at the bottom. This regional disparity in advertising is a corollary of different levels of economic and social development in China. Advertising is concentrated in three metropolitan cities: Beijing, Shanghai, and Guangzhou. Advertising revenues generated in these three cities account for half of the national total.[106]

The Chinese government has pushed for reform in the advertising business to establish it as a legitimate industry that contributes to economic development and protects consumer interests. The reform agenda called for developing an advertising industry represented by state-owned, private, and joint-venture agencies, adopting an agency system as the industry standard, setting up an advertising review process, and expediting the internationalization process of the advertising industry.[107] The goal of the last agenda was to introduce to the Chinese advertising market foreign capital, skills and techniques, and management experiences.

Foreign ads reappeared in *Wen Hui Bao,* a prominent Shanghai newspaper, and on Shanghai TV in March 1979. The first foreign product reintroduced to Chinese consumers through television advertising was the Swiss Rado wristwatch. The Rado campaign, brokered by the Hong Kong-based Gilman & Co., was structured around the theme of Rado being the modernized watch, designed to echo the "Four Modernizations" program which underpinned China's economic reform movement.[108] The impact of the campaign was overwhelming. It stimulated Chinese consumers' interest in the product even though it was way beyond their means to purchase it. The campaign not only showcased the history, philosophy, and technology of timekeeping but, more important, ushered the Chinese people into a brave new world of advertising and consumer goods.

By 1981 at least five multinational ad agencies had been actively engaged in discussing business opportunities with the Chinese government. These early arrivals included Dentsu, Young & Rubicam, McCann-Erickson, Ogilvy & Mather, and Leo Burnett.[109] The Japanese agency Dentsu was the first foreign ad agency to open offices in China in 1979. Despite little presence of their products in the Chinese market, Japanese companies used advertising to create brand awareness of Sony, National, Mitsubishi, Sanyo, and their electronic products and appliances.[110] The U.S. agency McCann-Erickson formed a joint venture with Jardine Matheson & Company, a Hong Kong trading firm, and became the first Western ad agency to establish a representative office in China.[111] Young & Rubicam initiated efforts to promote Chinese products overseas with funding from both Chinese exporters and U.S. importers.[112] Ogilvy & Mather signed agreements with local Chinese agencies to represent Chinese products in the world markets as well as international accounts such as American Express, Rado watch, Boeing, and Phillips television in China.[113] In general, in those early years, foreign ad agencies mostly handled their businesses through their Asia Pacific regional offices in Hong Kong.

As its "sleeping ad market wakes up,"[114] foreign ad agencies have grown increasingly enthusiastic about entering China. Major players in global advertising, such as J. Walter Thompson and Saatchi & Saatchi, have followed suit and set up shops in mainland China. J. Walter Thompson stated in its advertising, "At J. Walter we've made China business our business."[115] An ad for Leo Burnett said, "These days every advertising agency is talking about doing business in China. But the big question is, who can deliver?" It continued, "Since we've brought up these questions, you've probably guessed that the answers will point to us. So, to make things easy, just call us at Leo Burnett and we'll give you the details."[116]

The Chinese reform came to a sudden halt after the government crackdown of the student-led protest in Beijing in spring 1989. In the wake of the incident and amidst Western political leaders' condemnation of the Chinese government, the multinational companies kept a low profile but generally continued their business with China or inside the country.[117] The Chinese government reiterated its commitment to open policies and economic reform. It did not take long before business in China reached a new momentum. Foreign advertising in China experienced a similar hiccup. The coverage of the trade publication *Advertising Age* immediately after the Tiananmen crackdown through 1992 serves as a good indicator of the mood and movement of foreign advertising in China during that period. In its June 12, 1989 issue, the front-page story was titled "China quake: New crackdown may shatter plans of Western marketers." A year later a story on Chinese advertising had the headline "Ads return to Chinese market."[118] Another story appearing later that same year compared advertising development between the former Soviet Union and China and was titled "Agency exec bullish on China."[119] China's ad boom finally appeared to be on its way to turning into a reality in 1992 with the headline "Agencies flock to China as market 'explodes.'"[120]

During the early 1990s, agencies Grey, BBDO, and DDB Needham all formed joint ventures with local Chinese companies to conduct business inside the country. Since the Chinese market is too vast for one office to oversee, the global ad agencies use a divided market approach by setting up branch offices in Beijing, Shanghai, and Guangzhou, which cover North China, East China, and South China, respectively. The primary motive of these multinational agencies to enter China was to provide service to their international clients who had started to cultivate the large consumer market there.[121] As the Chinese consumer market grew stronger, profitability had also become a big concern in entering the China market.[122] The entry strategies of foreign ad agencies included setting up joint ventures with local Chinese companies or representative offices, or doing business on a project basis via Hong Kong.

Table 2.3 shows five of the leading global ad agencies' affiliates in Beijing in spring 1996. Three of them established joint ventures with Chinese partners. The foreign partners have majority stockholding (BBDO 51%, DDB Needham 61%, Grey 70%), which also confers management control in the joint ventures. The other two agencies (DMB&B and Leo Burnett) had set up representative offices in the capital city of China. At the time, they were headed by a team of overseas expatriate managers from Hong Kong, Singapore, the United States, and Denmark. Their

Table 2.3 Selected multinational advertising agencies in Beijing in 1996

Agency	World rank 1995	Year established	Foreign investment	Major accounts
BBDO	5	Early 90s	Joint venture (51%)	Apple Computer, Bayer, Sara Lee, Volvo
Leo Burnett	6	1995	Representative office (100%)	Philip Morris, McDonald's, United Airlines, Carlsburg
DDB Needham	7	1992	Joint venture (61%)	Henkle, Volkswagen, Audi
Grey	8	1992	Joint venture (70%)	Smithkline Beecham, Nokia, Goldstar, P&G
DMB&B	17	1991	Representative office (100%)	Mars, GM, Bausch & Lomb

Sources: Interviews with advertising executives in Beijing, Spring 1996. 1995 world rank from *Advertising Age,* April 15, 1996, p. s15.

major clients were international companies, such as Proctor & Gamble, Apple Computer, Philip Morris, McDonald's, Mars, and Volkswagen. They had not yet sought out local Chinese clients. For local accounts, they generally operated on a project basis.

There are several reasons why foreign ad agencies have primarily focused on international accounts.[123] First, these agencies generally entered the Chinese market with their international clients. The local Chinese agencies still lack the experience and expertise in working with multinational companies. The foreign agencies, on the other hand, have a much better understanding of the marketing needs of international companies. Second, the parallel pricing system, under which the advertising rates for foreign goods are much higher than for domestic products, makes foreign advertising more profitable. Agencies can earn higher incomes from working on international accounts. Third, the Chinese advertisers (with a few exceptions) do not yet seem to appreciate the role of an ad agency in their marketing efforts. They are therefore reluctant to turn their accounts over to the foreign agencies and spend much money on advertising research and execution.

But this is certainly changing. More and more Chinese domestic advertisers have started to seek out multinational agencies to design and implement advertising and promotion for them. The Guangdong-based electronic appliance manufacturer Kelon handed its entire account to Leo Burnett. According to one report, Chinese domestic clients accounted for half the billings at the Chinese branch of Ogilvy & Mather.[124]

The total revenue generated by these agencies increased from 0.3 billion yuan in 1992 to 1.8 billion yuan in 1996. Despite its visibility, foreign advertising still makes up only a small portion of the total advertising revenue in China, about 5% in 1996.[125] It has not been very profitable either, due to, for example, the high overheads and high costs of stationing expatriates in China. An article that appeared in the Hong Kong-based trade publication *Media* in August 1993 captured some of the frustrations that the international agencies had been experiencing as they started to explore the Chinese market:[126]

> Foreign agencies and clients are leaping at the chance to enter the China market, such is its promise and potential. Yet non-Chinese agencies suffer indignities and constraints for very little reward. They are compelled by official requirements to enter a joint-venture arrangement, to pay outrageous joint-venture or foreign media rates, to run offices at a loss for years and to take backward steps to the very basics of advertising in techniques—all because China is still not ready for the complexities and sophistication of advertising of the rest of Asia.

Nonetheless, these multinational companies have since established a strong foothold and made significant inroads into the Chinese market. They seem to believe that China is their long-term investment and that their patience and perseverance will pay off eventually.

Conclusion

If China's first exposure to foreign consumer products and advertising culture occurred in the 1920s and 1930s, the 1990s may well prove to be China's second major encounter with global consumer culture. Only this time, its experience is more massive and far-reaching. As for foreign advertisers and ad agencies, they again find themselves intrigued by the prospect of selling one bar of soap or one can of Coke to every Chinese, but also challenged by the daunting task of persuading a people with a long, distinguished history and tradition to change their habits of mind and of living. At least the "statistical extravaganza" has become even more spectacular, from a potential market of 400 million in the 1930s to that of more than one billion in the 1990s. What's more, as one expatriate ad executive put it, "It is an extremely rewarding experience to take huge international brands to China, market them from scratch, and see how well they do in China after a couple of years. I doubt if anyone will ever have such opportunities again."[127]

3

Modern Temptation: The Siren Songs of Consumption in Foreign Ads

Advertising has become a fixture in modern cities. "If one thinks about the social impact of advertising," as Daniel Bell pointed out, "its most immediate, yet usually unnoticed, consequence has been to transform the physical center of the city."[1] It is now virtually impossible for a city dweller to live a day without any advertising exposure. Like their counterparts in the West, urban Chinese are also living in a kaleidoscopic advertising environment.

Mary Douglas and Baron Isherwood have convincingly argued that goods do not merely possess utilitarian values but instead "commodities are good for thinking: treat them as a nonverbal medium for the human creative faculty."[2] Advertisements are the vehicles through which meanings are generated, expressed, and legitimized. Aside from describing features and functions of products and services, advertising also reflects, constructs, and communicates social mores and cultural values. Advertising, according to Jackson Lears, is a "symbolic universe where certain values were sanctioned and others rendered marginal or invisible."[3] Advertising plays no less a small part in shaping and reinforcing our collective beliefs and sensibilities.

The cultural significance of advertising thus compels us to scrutinize the appearances and representations in advertisements. As Leo Lee has put it, "We must not neglect the 'surfaces'—images and styles that do not necessarily enter into the depth of thought but nevertheless conjure up a collective 'imaginary.'"[4] For example, American advertisements can reveal, Jib Fowles argued, "many of the inner workings and secret protocols of American culture."[5] In a similar vein, the social tableaux in the foreign advertisements in China also document a rich history of Chinese consumers' encounters with modern consumer culture. They are the sites where the cultural signification of foreign products is realized and communicated in the new marketplace. When foreign products and brand names first entered this new, unfamiliar Chinese cultural space, they were facing the daunting challenge of establishing a meaningful relationship with their prospective customers who had a rather different history and culture. As shown in Chapter 3, advertising was and is the focal point of interpretation for Chinese consumers in their everyday world of goods in the early part of the century as well as in the 1980s and 1990s.

This chapter examines the "structure of attention" in selected foreign advertisements. To provide an overview of the landscape of foreign ads in contemporary urban China, the chapter begins with a brief discussion of the rise of consumerism since the economic reform in the late 70s and the 80s. It is followed by a three-part study.

The first part describes a survey of the advertising environment on a typical day in Beijing.[6] This snapshot survey aims to shed some light on the everyday advertising environment.

The second part examines one of the defining motifs in foreign advertisements in China—a sense of modernity. Advertising is a prime purveyor of social identity in the consumption process.

So, what kind of modern identity is embodied in foreign ads circulated in the Chinese media environment? What sort of ideals do these ads try to convince Chinese consumers to desire and to identify with? In short, this section attempts to show that advertising is one of the cultural forums where modernity and, more important, the pursuit of modernity is legitimized and idealized.

In part three, a focus group discussion demonstrates how Chinese consumers may receive and reconstitute cultural elements in foreign ads in the context of their everyday lives.

The Consumer Revolution

"While not every country is capable of becoming a consumer society in the near future," observed Francis Fukuyama, "there is hardly a society in the world that doesn't embrace the goal itself."[7] As stated by the Chinese government over the years, the fundamental purpose of the economic reform in China is to increase national wealth. The Chinese government has emphasized the production of goods and the improvement of people's living standard, but has not claimed to move the country toward a consumer society. Rather, from the outset, a consumer society was cast in the Chinese media as a culture full of wasteful habits, money chasing, and worship of material possessions.[8] The government has launched sporadic limited campaigns to denounce conspicuous consumption among the *nouveaux riches*. Despite a higher savings rate than in many other countries, the increase in disposable income (nearly tripled from 1985 to 1992) has awakened people's desires for consumption and material pleasures.

Material consumption is socially and historically constructed. Even the word "consumption" has evolved from a negative connotation of depletion to a more positive sense of enjoying life's pleasures.[9] It was not long ago that Chinese dressed in drab gray suits, and the cities were blighted with anonymous, concrete socialist blocks. A watch, bicycle, sewing machine, and transistor radio constituted the big four items that Chinese families had craved for nearly three decades up until the 1980s.[10] The entire country was then "consuming" not material goods but class politics. Years later the hyper-politicization of class struggle during the Mao Zedong era would be condemned as disastrous for the country's economic development.

In the late 1970s, economic development replaced class struggle as the nation's top priority. The traditional big four consumer items were quickly superseded by the new "big four"—washing machine, color TV, refrigerator, and tape recorder. In recent years this standard package has expanded to include piano, car, telephone, private apartment, air-conditioner, and personal computer.

Advertising is one visible aspect of the culture of consumption. It is, in Daniel Bell's characterization, "the mark of material goods, the exemplar of new styles of life, the herald of new values."[11] The role of foreign advertising in the cultural canonization of consumerism in China is indisputable. While the economic function of foreign advertising is quite obvious, the recurring motifs of material pleasures and modernity associated with the advertised products also perform a critical social and cultural function. Foreign advertising has reinforced, if not introduced, the new meaning of a good life to Chinese people. This second coming of foreign advertising and consumer culture signals the historical reversal of the hyper-politicization of communist ideology during the first decades of the PRC.

A Day in the Advertising Environment in Beijing

Advertising is now pervasive in China. It has transformed the look of the Chinese city from a deserted commercial wasteland to a thriving consumer wonderland. Constantly flashing out their invitations to buy, the neon lights illuminate and brighten the city. To capture some instructive glimpses of advertising in the contemporary cityscape in China, I surveyed the advertising environment (newspapers, magazines, TV, radio, outdoor billboards, and the subway) in Beijing on a day in spring 1996.[12] Although this may not represent a typical case, advertising in the capital city does provide some significant indications concerning the direction that advertising development is taking in China.

A total of 386 ads made up the advertising environment for

this snapshot survey. The survey revealed that almost 60% of the ads were for local products, while a little less than 40% were for foreign products. Foreign advertising was not evenly distributed in all of the media vehicles. It was featured most prominently in subway panel posters, taking up almost three-fourths of the total number of panels, and on outdoor billboards, which had twice as many foreign ads as local ones. Foreign advertising had relatively little presence in newspapers and on TV, where only about one in every four ads was for a foreign product.

In their study of advertising in Beijing during one week in October 1985, Sally Stewart and Nigel Campbell examined advertisements in four types of media—television, radio, newspapers, and billboards—and found little foreign advertising. For instance, during that week, *The People's Daily* and *The Economic Daily* printed 50 and 52 ads, respectively, of which only four and five in each were foreign ads. They did not hear any foreign ads on the radio during that week even though, according to their calculation, there were about 12 to 13 minutes of advertising time each day. Only 13 TV commercials were for foreign products on CCTV and Beijing TV during that week. Furthermore, they found only 14 foreign ads out of the 114 billboards they examined.[13] In short, despite the different time frames between the two snapshots, it does seem apparent that there were substantially more foreign ads in the media environment in 1996 than 10 years earlier.

Images and promises of consumer goods now permeate the advertising world. People come into contact with them on their way to work as well as during their leisure time at home. The majority of the ads in our snapshot survey were for consumer products, such as soft drinks, beer, snacks, fast food, TV, VCR, stereo, over-the-counter medicine, shampoo, soap, and detergent. About a quarter of the foreign ads were for food and beverages, and another one fifth for electronic and electric appliances, followed by cosmetics and apparel. In local advertising on the other hand, pharmaceutical products, food and beverages, and electronic/electric appliances were among the largest advertisers.

Chinese consumers are also becoming increasingly brand

conscious thanks to advertising, and they are sharing with consumers from around the world the same international brand names. Some of the advertised brands that one would have seen while walking down the street or travelling by subway in Beijing on that spring day in 1996 included Coca-Cola, McDonald's, Nestle, Beck's, Evian, Philips, Panasonic, Toshiba, Sharp, Colgate, Lux, Pantene, Kodak, Fuji, Goodyear, and Shell. Among these brands, Lux, Colgate, and Kodak were a few of the enduring brands that had first appeared in the Chinese media back in the 1920s and 1930s. They had staged a successful comeback after disappearing for three decades during the Chinese experiment of orthodox communism that effectively chased out foreign advertisers and uprooted the consumerist lifestyle.

Among the major advertisers, the U.S.-based corporations led the way. A total of 15 foreign countries were identified as the country of origin of a product or service in the survey. In terms of the number of ads, U.S. products were the most advertised, with Japan and Germany in second and third place. It is hardly surprising that the three powerhouses of the world economy also maintained a strong advertising presence in the largest potential market of China. However, a decade before, according to Stewart and Campbell's study, the little foreign advertising found in Beijing was predominantly for Japanese products, with very few European or U.S. advertisers.[14] The changing makeup of the advertising marketplace served as an indicator of the growing diversification and, most likely, the intensifying competition in the Chinese market environment.

Advertising Modernity

Whether it is called a fable or a parable, each advertisement is in essence a narrative.[15] Advertisements become communicative through the (re)arrangement of everyday happenings and their modes of expressions. One of the distinct features of advertising, as compared with other narratives, is that advertising, with few exceptions, tries to tell a happy/success story and to avoid unpleasant texts and images. Neither does the value of advertising narrative rest on its verisimilitude or authenticity to everyday reality; it is in fact mostly independent of reality. Advertising is after all a fantasy, a dream. One of the recurring motifs in foreign ads in China is the narrative of modernity.

The intellectual discourse on modernity is vast, from diagnosis of the mode of industrial production and bureaucratic organization in a capitalist political economy to analysis of the advancement of science and technology and its transformative impact on foundational beliefs in the society. Is modern life, as Marshall Berman has argued, inherently paradoxical and contradictory?[16] Is the modern era the age of the grand narrative of progress? Anthony Giddens gave a simple geographical and temporal definition of modernity, which refers to "modes of social life or organization which emerged in Europe from about the seventeenth century onwards and which subsequently became more or less worldwide in their influence."[17] To Daniel Bell, modernity in the appearance of artistic modernism presents "an extraordinary puzzle." Its "single cultural temper, movement—its very amorphousness or protean nature precludes a single encapsulating term—has persisted for more than a century and a quarter, providing renewed and sustained attacks on the social structure."[18] The modernity we are concerned with in this study centers around only several themes underlying modern sentiments: the pursuit of pleasure, novelty, technology, and Western-ness.

The Ethic of Pleasure

The worldview of consumerism has two dimensions. First, consumerism refers to the quest for material comfort instead of spiritual rewards.[19] Daniel Bell argued that hedonism—the idea of pleasure as a way of life—is the cultural, if not moral, justification of capitalism, and it has resulted in such sharp contrast to the ascetic beliefs embodied by American Puritanism—a constant struggle between "work and achieve" and "spend and enjoy."[20] Such consumerism is evident in developed and developing countries alike. However, the difference probably lies in that, unlike in developed countries where consumerism presupposes relative material affluence, consumerism in a subsistence economy co-exists with abject poverty.[21] The second dimension of consumerism, as we have argued earlier, is that commodities are purchased not for their intrinsic and functional utility but largely for their symbolic value or social status.[22] The manifestation of consumption for identity is found in developing as well as developed countries. These two dimensions of consumerism are often intertwined and inseparable.

It is commonplace that foreign ads extol the virtues of being comfort-seeking and fun-loving and how the advertised products would enable consumers to enjoy the pleasures of life.[23] Many of the foreign ads in two daily newspapers in China from 1985 to 1993 seem like variations of General Electric's "We bring good things to life" tagline. The ads for Toshiba, for instance, claim that their electronic appliances are able to enrich people's lives and enhance their satisfaction. One of the Toshiba ads contends that life is not yet convenient and comfortable if people merely own electronic appliances because they should also desire the kind of quality and beauty as exemplified by Toshiba.

The motifs of family and fun are evoked in a number of the foreign ads. Several brands of *karaoke* players were also heavily advertised during this period. *Karaoke* (sing-along), a pastime originated in Japan in the early 1980s, caught on in mainland China in the 1990s. The Panasonic *karaoke* ad depicts the product in a family setting, and its text reads, "Tonight the whole family get together and let's enjoy *karaoke*." The "family," which includes parents and grandparents, sit on the couch and enjoy a little girl's singing, with two other adults (presumably family friends or relatives) standing nearby and talking to each other. The happy, harmonious, and relaxing family scene also appears in the Casio electronic piano ad, in which the young and beautiful "wife" plays the instrument, with the good-looking "husband" standing closely behind her and three adorable children singing merrily beside them.

The Chinese youth are increasingly being socialized through the mass media into the global teenage culture. The Aiwa *karaoke* player ad idealizes a fun-loving life for the Chinese youth by depicting energetic Chinese-looking adolescents in flashy clothes enthusiastically singing *karaoke*. "Now you can watch and sing; Aiwa provides the most enjoyment."

The ads preach and reiterate that life's gratification will be boundless with the purchase of the advertised products. Consumer products are elevated to become the chief sources of comfort, pleasure, and fun in the Chinese people's everyday reality.

New, New, New

Modernity in China is generally understood as representing rapid economic development and growing availability of consumer goods. It is associated with and embodied in products that are new, technological, and, above all, Western. One of the sales pitches in China is to identify with what is "modern."

The narrative of modernity emphasizes a continuous temporal break with the past and is keen on the now and the present. The relentless pursuit of novelty has given rise to the pervasive usage of the word "new." Similar to advertisements in the West, foreign ads in China also highlight products' "newness." Such hackneyed phrases and adjectives as "a new generation," "newer," "more advanced," and "latest" are omnipresent. The word "new" must be truly the most overworked term in the advertising lexicon.[24]

TV sets were one of the main staples in foreign ads during the study period of 1985-1993. TV sets advertised in the 1990s were promoted for their larger screen and better sound and picture quality than their older models. The "The One Up" campaign for Panasonic TV emphasizes the "up" part of the theme. Its Chinese equivalent of "The One Up" is "The New Picture King," and "new" is highlighted in the advertising copy.

The strategy to emphasize the improved model of TV could be a direct response to the expansion of the television market in China during the second half of the 1980s. In 1985, less than 7% of the Chinese population owned a TV set. But in 1992 almost 20% of the population had TV sets at home and the penetration rate was much higher in urban China.[25] By promoting the upgraded products, these ads served as a constant reminder that to be modern is to be forever at the forefront of what's "new."

Culture of Technology

To be modern also means to embrace the culture of technology. As has been articulated by the Chinese government, one important component of the Four Modernizations program is the modernization of science and technology. The consensus reached in China as to why the country, with a brilliant and glorious past, now lags behind many developed countries is that science and technology has not been fully developed and widely applied. As part of the official ideology, science and technology is indisputably one of the defining themes of modernity in China.

The foreign ads in Chinese newspapers tout technological advances in consumer products. For instance, the Sharp VCR ads describe, in meticulous detail, its technological component and advancement. One ad displays in large boldface the name of the metal the VCR head is made of. It is doubtful, however, whether consumers can make any sense of why that metal can improve the performance of a Sharp VCR. In another Sharp ad, the advertised VCR is made transparent and affords consumers a good look at its technically complex inside. The message of technology is once again pronounced.

The unfamiliar jargon, technical data, and engineering features help create the aura of advanced technology. By mystifying the product, the techno-speech eventually translates into consumers' perception of product superiority.[26] The motif of technology is quite extensively used to capitalize on China's thirst and quest for technological modernity, and the culture of technology is, as a result, glorified.

White and Western

In China, perhaps as anywhere else in the developing world, the notion of modernity also implies one's ability to identify with the aspirations and practices of Western developed countries. Disillusioned by the lack of material development, many Chinese turn to worshipping anything that is "white" and Western. Therefore a product associated with elements of Western culture tends to have more appeal. This is clearly embodied in the prevalent use of very Westernized names and symbols for local products and their logos.

One of the advertising strategies to gratify Chinese consumers' desire for Western culture, or some "modernity," is the employment of Caucasian models in the ads. One Sharp TV ad pictures a Caucasian soccer player. Another Sharp stereo ad depicts a Caucasian conductor and a Caucasian violinist playing Beethoven's Sixth Symphony. The Casio portable TV ad features a good-looking Caucasian young man in four different situations where the portable TV can be used. The appeal of Caucasian imagery seems to even extend to the use of mixed-looking models with Eurasian features (e.g., the female in a Casio camera ad).

The plausible explanation for the employment of Caucasian models in these ads is that Chinese consumers are attracted to Western images, which signify to them an affluent, exotic "Other." Millie R. Creighton has cogently argued in her study of the advertising representation of Caucasians in Japan,[27]

> The social construction of *gaijin* denies the individual uniqueness of Westerners, transforming all Caucasians into an essentialized category that reduces the complex variations among them. Just as Western orientalism created self-occidentalisms through an implied contrast with a simplified West, Japanese renderings of *gaijin* are occidentalisms that stand opposed to Japanese orientalisms about themselves.

If the Banana Republic mail-order catalog in the United States makes people of color from the Third World seem exotic,[28] then the same argument can be extended to the use in the foreign ads in China of Caucasian models, who are the Chinese "Exotic Other." But, unlike Westerners' Third World Other, which is more likely to be impoverished but romanticized, the Western Other is represented and presented to the Chinese consumers as permanently affluent and advanced, and detached from its history of development.

To sum up, aside from their utilitarian functions, consumer products are endowed with cultural meanings to provide existential guidance. The foreign advertisements discussed here portrayed material pleasures as a desirable good life for the Chinese consumers. They affirmed that one of the ways to acquire an identity of modernity is to consume goods symbolized by newness, technology, and Western otherness.

Foreign Ads in the Eyes of Chinese Consumers

Chinese consumers probably do not see "hidden persuasion" in advertising. They attach more importance to the perceived beneficial aspects of commercial advertising than to what might be termed its harmful dimension, a commonplace perception in developed markets. Chinese consumers, for instance, like to embrace advertising as a useful way to get to know a product better. So in general, advertising doesn't face as much resistance from the audience in this emerging market as in a mature market, such as the United States, where commercial avoidance has become routine. With an unsuspecting audience, this might prove to be the "golden age" for advertisers and ad agencies to develop and execute promotional strategies in China. This is particularly true with foreign advertising.

Marlboro Country: A Foreign Country Called America

Nothing typifies the favorable reception of foreign ads in China better than the Marlboro Country TV commercials and the cowboy billboards. Even though cigarette advertising is now officially banned in the broadcast and print media, the image of the Marlboro man, selected as the number one advertising icon of the 20th century by *Advertising Age* in 1999,[29] has achieved such a lasting impact that it has also become part of the collective consumer memory in Chinese society.

During a focus group discussion I held at a Shanghai vocational school in May 1996 on foreign advertising in the Chinese media,[30] one participant said:

> Normally when we turn on TV, we are not particularly interested in watching ads. We want to watch something with a story or a plot. Most people don't turn on TV to

> watch ads. If I turn on TV and see an ad, I will usually switch to a different channel. But if it is the Marlboro commercial, I won't. Because at the very first sight, I don't think it looks like a commercial. Rather, it is more like the beginning of a TV drama. So, I will continue watching. The Marlboro commercial just immediately grabs my attention.

Since all eight participants in the focus group enjoyed the Marlboro Country commercials, I asked them what they found so appealing. One participant replied, "It's the horse and the cowboy. The freedom and masculinity." "It presents us," another answered, "a landscape we don't have in China." One added, "The Marlboro commercial simply makes viewers very excited."

The motifs of virility, rugged individualism, and self-achievement evoked by the lone cowboy in the American wild West seemed to have struck a responsive chord in the Chinese psyche just as they had in the United States. Several participants also observed that the background music in the commercials enhanced the movements on the screen and stimulated audience emotion. The Marlboro ads seem to have tapped into an imagery, a mood or perhaps an attitude that apparently has a cross-cultural appeal. Surprisingly or unsurprisingly, none of the participants saw the "merchants of death" in the Marlboro Country.

As the focus group grew enthusiastic about discussing how impressed they were by the sense of freedom, independence, and masculinity conveyed in the Marlboro commercials, I posed the question, "What will it be like if we make an ad, using a lone Chinese horse-rider on the Inner Mongolia prairie, for instance? Will that achieve the same effect?" I further explained that it would not be difficult to find a similar landscape in China as a backdrop and that we would also try to maintain the same filming quality as in the original Marlboro ads. The question sent my participants into a moment of silence. Some said it would be a rather different ad. When I probed in what way it would be different, they were not able to articulate the perceived difference, but they could certainly feel it.

It appears that people in China approach the Marlboro ads with many pre-existing notions about the American West, the cowboy, and the American doctrine of self-reliance and individual freedom. In other words, the meaning of the Marlboro ads doesn't simply reside in the physical landscape or in the image of the cowboy. The landscape and the cowboy are only one aspect of this inter-textuality and are vehicles for Chinese audiences to validate their preconceived notions about America and its cultural essence. In the eyes of Chinese consumers, Marlboro Country is a foreign country called America. Watching the Marlboro commercials becomes a *de facto* vicarious cultural experience. Chinese consumers' curiosity and fascination with America—the country and its culture—were momentarily satisfied through the viewing of the stylized representations in these commercials.

Recalling Foreign Brand Names

The success of the creative execution in foreign ads is also manifested by the audience's impressive recall of foreign ads and brand names. During the focus group discussion, I asked each participant to quickly name three foreign product brands and their commercials. None of the participants seemed to have any difficulty in sharing their favorite foreign ads, from Coca-Cola and McDonald's to Nike and Energizer. The most mentioned were ads for baby hygiene products by Johnson & Johnson.

Then I asked them to name three local brands and their ads. After a somewhat longer interval of silence, one participant uttered one brand name. After some discussion, the group finally came up with three or four specific ads and brands.

This pattern of response was repeated when I asked them to name spokespersons in both foreign and domestic TV commercials. It appeared that they were much more familiar with celebrities from Hong Kong, Taiwan, the United States, and Japan, such as Andy Lau (Hong Kong pop singer), Jackie Chan (Hong Kong movie star), Michael Jordan (U.S. basketball star), Michael Chang (U.S. tennis star), and Cindy Crawford (U.S. supermodel), than with local Chinese celebrities in ads.

Admiring Foreign Ads

The overwhelming positive reception of the Marlboro ads perfectly exemplifies a sort of triumph of foreign advertising over local advertising in China. Said one participant,

> I find foreign ads more interesting. They are often humorous. For example, the ad for Energizer battery. It catches my attention. In local ads, actors are often shown, posing to explain what the product is. They are just boring and not exciting to watch.

Another participant explained why she liked foreign ads more than local ads:

> Local ads are plainspoken. They are difficult to get people's attention. Foreign ads are more exciting to watch. And, you also get enchanted when watching foreign ads (for instance the colorful commercial for Nippon Paint).

Two more observations from the focus group:

> It seems that foreign ads are able to highlight the functions of the product. I especially like the creativity in the ads. They are more playful and innovative.

> The content in foreign ads is brief and concise. Local ads are full of detailed information. We get overwhelmed by it.

The prevailing favorable attitude toward foreign advertising demonstrated during the focus group discussion is by no means unique to this group. A survey I conducted at the same school revealed that, of the 196 respondents, nearly 58% of the respondents held a positive view of foreign advertising.[31] Only two (3%) disliked foreign advertising. Asked whether their purchase decisions were influenced by advertising, most (70%) reported that advertising had some influence, and 15% said advertising had a tremendous influence on their purchasing decisions.

These results echo earlier research on Chinese attitudes toward foreign advertising. According to a 1987 survey by Richard W. Pollay, David K. Tse, and Zhangyuan Wang, foreign ads were perceived by Chinese consumers as "more honest, more artistically designed and a more pleasant experience," and "more memorable and more convincing."[32] A survey by the People's University of China and China Central TV in Beijing in 1987 indicated that almost 30% of the residents liked foreign advertising and more than 10% liked it very much.[33] Other surveys also showed that people with higher income and higher education, or the younger generation, tended to like foreign advertising more than those with less income and less education, or the older generations.[34] Chinese consumers thought foreign advertising could help increase their knowledge about foreign cultures and society. Foreign ads were also perceived to be more entertaining and creative than local advertising.[35]

The young Chinese consumers in the focus group apparently were not critical of foreign advertising. When I asked them about any negative aspect of foreign advertising, the participants replied they simply enjoyed foreign ads and had no objection to them. One participant did mention that the prices for foreign goods were prohibitively high for some consumers and that, for them, foreign ads probably would not be as attractive because they could not afford the goods in the ads.

A 1988 survey showed that some Chinese consumers found foreign advertising impractical, the reason being that the advertised goods were often not widely available in stores.[36] But this concern is no longer valid since the trickle of foreign consumer goods in the Chinese market then has now become a full stream. Few people in the focus group viewed foreign advertising as a stimulus to consumerism, a challenge to Chinese traditional values, or a form of cultural invasion. Instead, Chinese consumers seem to admire the Western subtle style of advertising and welcome the sophisticated advertising techniques practiced by multinational ad agencies.[37]

In short, among Chinese consumers, foreign advertising appears to be preferred over local advertising. Foreign ads are in general perceived as better than local ads in terms of creative concepts and execution. Chinese consumers are most impressed by the use of visuals and soundtracks in foreign ads. Chinese local ads pale in comparison to the "make-believe" quality in foreign advertising. More important, perhaps, aside from the overall superior production quality of foreign ads, what underlies Chinese consumers' overwhelming preference for foreign ads seems to be their curiosity about and yearning for the exotic and the affluent "Other," embodied by the stylized representations of lifestyles in the foreign ads.

4

Inside the Shop: A Case Study of a Multinational Ad Agency in Beijing

Like other media products, advertisements represent a constructed reality. They are cultural objects that embody socially and culturally (and sometimes politically) meaningful expressions.[1] But unlike other media products, without claims of authorship, advertising by and large remains anonymous. The glitz and glamour of commercials tend to disguise the politics in advertising production as well as consumption.

Ad agencies are the site of cultural production. When a foreign ad agency enters the Chinese market, does it basically reproduce or creatively adapt itself in the new social, economic, and cultural setting? This chapter addresses this issue by examining the transfer of a foreign ad agency to China. Focusing on a global advertising affiliate in Beijing (hereafter called the Agency),[2] it explores how the foreign organizational form gets translated and transformed into the Chinese environment. Specifically, it looks at three aspects of the social context of production at the Agency:

1. The structural design
2. The network of people within the Agency
3. The professional norms and values

The institutional design is a fundamental condition of the organization through which ads are produced and disseminated. It is also important to think of the Agency as a social organization—"a network of people who cooperate to produce that work"—rather than mere abstract structures.[3] Professional ideals set the standard for the practice of the trade and give the profession meaning and identity. To be sure, this description only partially covers the structure and process of the Agency. The emphasis is on how elements of the foreign and the local are negotiated and manifested in these three important aspects of the conditions of foreign advertising production.

The Setting

As China's capital for most of the last 500 years, Beijing has captured the imagination of foreigners as well as Chinese with its grand imperial architectural wonders. The economic reform since the late 1970s has helped transform the city's landscape. Beijing has taken on the new look of a teeming global metropolis.

The serenity of the majestic Forbidden City now coexists with the excitement of skyscrapers aggressively springing up around the city. Unlike the symbolic power of the magnificent architectural cluster of the Forbidden City, skyscrapers are "the product, by and large, of cultures that are in the first flush of excitement at moving onto the world stage," as Paul Goldberger pointed out. "Such buildings are assertions of power, demands to be noticed, and there is a particular moment in the life cycle of a rising culture when those impulses are irresistible. The moment comes after beginnings and before maturity."[4] Beijing is experiencing such a moment of modernization.

The Agency is located in one of those gleaming glass skyscrapers in the northeastern part of Beijing. Apparently on a par with international standards, this modern building, with amenities and conveniences, is a world away from the old quarters of the city. Walking into its lobby, it would be difficult to distinguish this building in Beijing from one located in Chicago. Besides the types of services an office tower normally provides, this one also has a cheerful flower shop, a pleasant mini-market, a fine Chinese restaurant, a Western café, and even a shower room especially designed for employees working in the building complex. The Agency is one of the many companies renting office space in this skyscraper.

The work environment at the Agency is similar to a typical corporate office in, for instance, the United States. The carpeted, clean, air-conditioned, brightly lit office has an open floor plan. Smoking is prohibited inside the office. Drinking water and coffee are provided free of charge. The office furniture has a simple but consistent style. The interior walls are decorated with the Agency's successful ad campaign posters. Awards and other professional recognition are also on display in the reception area.

The general manager works in an executive office with a panoramic view of the city. The deputy manager also has a private but slightly smaller office. For the rest of the employees, cubicles are their office space, with a desk, a chair, and a telephone. The heads of the divisions share the same open rooms with employees but have larger cubicles and desks. With a growing staff, the office space does look somewhat crowded.

The conference room is equipped with a TV, a slide projector, and a VCR. The TV set also receives satellite programming. During lunch breaks, employees often watch news or entertainment programs in the conference room. A private office is reserved for the exclusive use of visiting staff from other offices. Company computers, fax, and copy machines are all in the open area.

On a typical day, dial tones, busy signals, and other electronic signals emitted from telephones, fax machines, photocopiers, and computers form the constant background sound in the work environment. But, in the creative department, which occupies a separate office floor, soft music is usually playing, creating a different, more soothing atmosphere.

Organization of Work

The Agency, established in the early 1990s, is a joint venture between a Chinese ad company and one of the world's leading global ad agencies headquartered in the United States. Like other major players in global advertising, in addition to its Beijing office, the parent company has also set up operations in two other Chinese cities, Shanghai and Guangzhou.

The entry strategies of Western multinational ad agencies have taken three basic forms as they expand their services around the world:

1. A *brand agency,* where the overseas office is a local office or subsidiary of the parent multinational agency,
2. An *affiliate,* where the parent multinational agency has substantial but not 100% control of the overseas agency,
3. An *associate,* where the parent multinational agency is loosely or tightly connected to a local agency but has no official equity.[5]

The strategy of establishing an affiliate is an example of a joint-venture arrangement.

Under the economic liberalization policies in post-Mao China, the Chinese government has strongly encouraged foreign investment in China. There are generally three basic forms of foreign investment enterprises—equity joint venture, contractual joint venture, and wholly foreign-owned enterprises. Although it has come to agree upon the purpose and benefits of commercial advertising in its drive toward a market economy, the Chinese government also recognizes that advertising is more than an economic institution and that it wields enormous cultural and ideological power as well. The government still doesn't permit wholly foreign-owned advertising companies inside China to avoid the potential loss of control of this culture-influencing industry. As

Neil Fligstein argued, the production of market institutions is a "political-cultural project."[6] Thus, foreign agencies are only allowed to operate in China in the form of a joint venture.

The case of the Agency represents an equity joint venture. Equity joint ventures are "limited liability business associations in which the Chinese and foreign parties each take an equity share."[7] The managerial control in equity joint ventures is often determined by each party's capital contribution. In the case of the Agency, the foreign partner is the majority shareholder in the joint venture and therefore also has control over operation and management.

The general manager and division heads at the Agency are expatriates (hereafter "expats," as they are usually called in the field) appointed by the parent company's office in Hong Kong. The deputy manager is a local Chinese, representing the Chinese partner company. The Agency is in constant communication with the Hong Kong office but is loosely connected with the U.S. headquarters. Representatives from the headquarters do visit the Beijing office for internal audit, for instance. When working on a worldwide pitch for a product, the U.S. office may also contact the Beijing office for relevant information or assistance.

The expats run the day-to-day operation at the Agency. There is virtually no involvement of the Chinese partner in daily management matters. The Chinese deputy manager appears to be only a nominal figure in this context. He oversees some company logistics, such as dealing with the local bureaucracy. When he first assumed the position, he asked the foreign management to assign him some tasks. But apparently the foreign management did not want much involvement from its local partner. Besides the deputy manager, two other local staff are also slated for some management responsibilities in their respective media and administrative divisions.

The foreign majority shareholding and managerial governance are ways to minimize potential conflicts between the partners in a joint-venture business arrangement. If the experience of other companies is any indication, it seems that such a model is more feasible and desirable than the split-control model. When both the Chinese and foreign parties share equal management responsibilities, much confusion results due to the fundamental differences in business philosophy and practice between the partners. Protracted and incessant dissent in management can be a source of low morale in the workplace. For the foreign partner, the managerial control is also important in that, since wholly foreign ownership is out of the question at this point, such a mechanism of control ensures that its corporate culture will not be diluted in the new context. Overall, cooperation and communication between the foreign management and the local company have been based on an understanding of each one's role in the joint venture, with the local influence in management being kept to a minimum.

The Agency mostly services foreign businesses in the Chinese market, many of which are blue-chip accounts. The Agency offers its clients a full range of marketing and promotional services, from planning and producing advertising and promotions to conducting advertising research, selecting, purchasing, and monitoring media. Like any standard full-service agency, the Agency has three major departments: account service, media, and creative. It also has a small administrative staff and an adjunct division of health product promotion.

The standard description of the account service, media, and creative departments in a full-service agency in Western advertising is also reflected in the structure and function of the three major departments at the Agency. The *account service department* is the key link in the agency-client relationship and the agency business activities. The Agency has nine account service employees, three of whom are account managers and are in charge of specific clients with the assistance of account executives. At any given time they may be simultaneously responsible for several accounts. The general manager also serves as the supervisor of the account service.

The *media department* is the liaison between the client and the communication media. It, for instance, gathers/generates media rating and competition reports, and provides media monitoring. The Agency's media department, with a staff of nine, performs three different functions: media planning, buying, and monitoring. This department is headed by an expat. Another expat works on media planning and a local Chinese supervises media buying and monitoring.

The *creative department* oversees the creation of the advertisements. The copywriter writes the headlines, subheads, and body copy; the art director and the graphic artist are responsible for designing the layouts and execution. The Agency has one copywriter, three graphic artists, and a production executive. The director of the department is dispatched from Hong Kong. The Hong Kong office also periodically sends over art directors on special projects.

In addition, the *administrative branch,* which includes secretaries, accountants, and public relations coordinator, maintains the day-to-day operation of the entire office. As one of its major clients is a pharmaceutical company, the Agency also has a two-member team working on direct marketing of healthcare products to doctors and hospitals.

A typical process of advertising planning and production begins with the account service receiving instructions from a client on product marketing goals and plans. The account staff generate a brief, which details marketing objectives, target audience, and other relevant market information. The brief is then shared with the media and creative departments.

The media department articulates its own objectives in terms of how to reach target consumers via selected advertising media. The media staff make recommendations about the types of media and the amount of media time or space deemed appropriate for the proposed advertising campaign. Of critical importance is proposing a media budget that must be based on sound rationale and adequate analysis of the media and the market.

In the meantime, the creative staff have their own brainstorming sessions about ideas and concepts for the campaign. Their task is to make recommendations about creative executions, such as headlines, body copy, or a storyboard for a television commercial.

The process of planning and executing an ad campaign is seldom a one-way or one-step process. It involves constant negotiation and modification between the Agency and the client as well as among the three sections of the Agency. The account service staff coordinate the Agency efforts throughout the process. The media people inform and update the account executives about media booking. There are times, for instance, when the Agency fails to purchase the desired time slot or space, and the advertising plan needs to be adjusted. When the creative staff come up with a storyboard for a TV spot, it is forwarded to the media staff. The media department sends it to the advertising review board at the Chinese Advertising Association (CAA) for what the Agency people call the "censorship" procedure (*see* Chapter 5). Often the Agency needs to modify its proposed ad and resubmit to CAA for review again.

Once the Agency receives the final approval from CAA, the creative department enters the production stage. The Agency normally prepares print ads in-house. For TV commercials, production often takes place in Hong Kong because of the high-quality production facilities there. Sometimes the Agency hires a local production company in China and has post-production done in Hong Kong.

When the final ads are ready, the media department is responsible for delivering tapes or print copies to media outlets. The last gatekeepers in this process are the advertising media. They review all ads to be broadcast or printed. After the ads reach the media, the media department starts to monitor the media to ensure that the ads go on the air or appear in print according to the contract. The Agency's ads finally enter the advertising environment, competing for the attention of Chinese consumers.

The Network of People

The Workforce

With an average age of 25, the staff of the Agency are young and energetic. The educational background of the Agency staff varies from department to department. The account service requires college education and in particular a good command of English. Since the Agency mostly handles international accounts, its account executives are required to have strong communication skills in order to succeed on the job. College education is not viewed as important in the media and creative departments. Those staff often do not work directly with international clients, and therefore the company does not emphasize English proficiency and higher education background as much. More important, perhaps, "if we set our educational qualifications too high for every department," says the general manager, "we would not be able to find enough people to fill all these positions." The basic skills needed for media purchasing and monitoring can be learned on the job fairly easily and quickly. For the creative side, the graphic artists need to have specific training in drawing or design, normally acquired in an art college in China.

Some of the Agency staff were hired fresh from college. Others made their career moves to advertising from various other fields, such as journalism, sales, and marketing. For example, before joining the Agency, one of the media plan executives worked in a government agency for a year. Most of the staff entered the profession without much formal training in advertising.

The influence of commercial advertising was largely broken during the first decades of the People's Republic. The pressing need for local professionals has propelled the development of advertising education. China's first Department of Advertising was only established at Beijing Broadcasting Institute in 1992. Many colleges and universities are now offering advertising courses and programs. In 1996 there were no formal training programs in place at the Agency. The local staff basically learned the trade on the job.

A few have had previous experience in advertising. One of the account managers first worked at another multinational ad agency in Beijing immediately after college. That agency had earned a reputation as a training ground for Chinese advertising professionals. Her "apprenticeship" there made her one of the first generation of Chinese ad agents schooled in Western professionalism after the reintroduction of advertising to China in the late 1970s. The prior experience of the copywriter at the Agency involved a stint with another joint-venture agency in Beijing.

The expats at the Agency are dispatched from the Hong

Kong office. The general manager, for instance, was originally from Hong Kong and graduated from a North American school. His first position was as an account executive at the Agency's Hong Kong office. Later he left advertising and explored a career in marketing, trading, and outdoor media. Years later, after returning to the Agency's Hong Kong office, he again worked in the account service department until he began to lead the Beijing office.

Socialization at Work

The workday at the Agency begins at 8:30 in the morning. The management does not seem to be rigid about employees' work schedules. Lunch break is at noon. Business lunches are frequent. When there are no such engagements, staff have their lunch at the cafeteria in the building complex. Lunch coupons are provided by the firm as part of the staff benefits. After lunch they often take a nap in their cubicle, play games on the computer, watch TV in the conference room, or stroll outside the office tower. Work resumes around 1:00 or 1:30.

The expats usually arrive in the office somewhat later than the rest of the staff. They do not go to the employee cafeteria for lunch. Although the workday ends at 5:30, more often than not they stay later and also work weekends. Overtime is not compensated except that the company pays for meals and other expenses incurred by working extra hours.

The world of advertising is known for its informality in attire. There is no specified dress code at the Agency. Male employees typically wear shirts and slacks, and females wear blouses and skirts or dresses. Jeans and T-shirts are common as well. The account service staff are usually more formally dressed than the rest because they often meet with clients. The expats (except art directors) always dress more formally.

Language is another important aspect of Agency life. There is a constant lingual mix of Mandarin, Cantonese, and English, with Mandarin as the dominant language. Mandarin Chinese, based on the Beijing dialect, is the national language of the People's Republic. Cantonese is a dialect from southern China and is the prevalent language spoken in Hong Kong. For northerners in China, Cantonese sounds as foreign as English. English has become more or less the *lingua franca* of international business.

At any moment in the office one can hear these three languages. Most of the expats at the Agency try to speak Mandarin. When they talk to each other they normally speak in Cantonese, which local employees generally don't understand. English is often used between expats and locals, and between agency executives and client representatives. Even among local employees, some key phrases in advertising are invariably expressed in English, such as "rate card," "media reach," and "frequency." The computer database is mostly in English as well. It is now common for Chinese who work in international companies to adopt Western first names. One generally can hear conversations in Chinese peppered with English words and phrases.

At a meeting attended by a client representative of an international company, an account manager, and art directors, the client representative explained to the art directors why he did not like the ad they had produced for his product. During the exchanges among the four people, Mandarin, Cantonese, and English were all used. On another occasion, staff from the regional office in Hong Kong came to make a presentation. The presentation was interrupted several times because the presenter's Mandarin was not good enough and needed translation help from the staff in Beijing.

Language is one of the most fundamental aspects of culture that affect how we define and perceive ourselves as well as others. The mixture of languages at the Agency constantly reminds the expats and the local staff of their international and local identities.

The internal communication at the Agency is achieved in two basic ways: spoken communication and internal memo. The size of the office makes it possible for employees to talk to one another face-to-face most of the time. When the management wants to share something with the staff, it issues memos. Sometimes the memos are posted on a company bulletin board near the fax and copy machines.

Meaning of Work

Work often means more than paid employment. Aside from "earning a living," work has a psychological component as well. For the local staff, working at the Agency is meaningful at several levels. Employees at the Agency are paid a decent salary by the Chinese standard. The pay range varies according to one's experience, education, and position. The work environment at the Agency is certainly far superior than most of the state sector in China. The Agency's location in a modern office tower provides the kinds of amenities beyond the reach of most of the local companies.

On another level there is a certain element of prestige associated with working for a joint-venture company in contemporary Chinese society. Working at the Agency means being able to learn from the "real pros" in the advertising business. Even though working for a local agency can sometimes be financially more rewarding because of the practice of kickbacks, several local staff pointed out that the Agency provided a better opportunity for them to develop skills and attributes for the advertising profession.

For one of the local graphic designers, working at the Agency has been quite a learning process. His college education was in computer-assisted design and his previous work experience involved a similar position but at a local agency. While working at the Chinese ad agency he was given freedom and responsibility in designing ads. But at the Agency he works under the expat art director who oversees the creative strategy and execution. He has lost much control over the creation of an ad design. However, working at the Agency has been "a great learning experience, where I am exposed to the creative ideas of the experienced expats and the Western way of making advertising."

For some local staff, working at the Agency represents a change of pace from working in the state sector. Beyond teaching advertising skills, the Agency embodies a different work ethic and corporate culture. The workplace is imbued with energy and purpose, whereas much of the state sector tends to be full of lethargy, which often does more to inhibit one's development of professional potential than help nurture and develop it. Several local staff remarked that they came to work at the Agency to seek change and an opportunity to realize self-worth.

Before joining the Agency, one media executive worked at a government agency. The overwhelming lethargy at the workplace left her unmotivated. The Agency has been a welcome change. With no previous experience in advertising, she has been learning everything on the job and doesn't seem to mind the fact that since joining the Agency she has been working late and often on weekends.

If there is any complaint about working at the Agency, it is the constant pressure associated with meeting deadlines. The copywriter likes her current job except when she is asked to create appropriate prose within a very limited amount of time.

The expats often work long hours, including many weekends. The local staff are dismayed by such a work style. "The foreign management," says one local employee, "is sometimes heartless in their drive to work." Those who work closely with the expats have to also commit themselves to the work rhythm of the expats.

One account manager finds advertising an exciting, rewarding profession for young people seeking adventure and fulfillment, despite the constant pressure. "The advertising profession at times can be extremely demanding," she says, "and I will eventually quit advertising when I feel I've burnt out." Now, she seems to enjoy the excitement in the flourishing business.

The relationship between the expats and the locals at the Agency embodies an administrative as well as a professional hierarchy. For the local staff, working at the Agency becomes part of a learning process, and for the expats, a teaching process. Their roles are clearly defined and reinforced in their daily socialization at the Agency. However, the learning and teaching roles are not fixed and are sometimes reversed between the locals and the expats when the expats depend on the locals for cultural knowledge of the Chinese market to carry out advertising campaigns.

The Cultural Brokers

Standing in between the global manufacturer and the Chinese consumer, the Agency makes advertising of global products for local consumption. It therefore plays the role of a cultural broker in the transaction of advertising between the global and the local.

The parent company relies on the expats to maintain its operation and service quality in China. The expats at the Agency advise and supervise the production of advertising. They seem to have a better understanding of the needs of international advertisers. But their knowledge of the local cultural conditions is limited. They depend on the local staff for cultural information to achieve authenticity in advertising messages. In this sense the expats and the locals are mutually complementary in creating "an effective juncture" between the foreign product and the Chinese consumer.[8]

The expat art directors work closely with local employees, for example. Taking into account the huge size of the country and the cultural differences among different regions within China, the Agency often needs to design various versions of the same ad to cater to the regional markets in the country. It is therefore imperative for the expats to communicate with the locals in order to arrive at the appropriate language and image for a specific region.

One of the responsibilities of the local copywriter at the Agency is to make sure that the expressions in the headlines and body copy of the ads are acceptable and understandable in mainland China. Although mainland Chinese and overseas Chinese share the same Chinese language, some grammatical and syntactic differences are often obvious. Therefore, when ad copy or storyboards arrive from the Agency's Hong Kong office, the copywriter edits them to ensure the correct sentence structure and diction. For example, two Chinese characters—"zeng" and "song"—make up the Chinese phrase "gift giving." In Hong Kong it is customarily expressed as "song zeng." But in Mainland China the phrase is "zeng song." Even though local Chinese can still understand the meaning of the phrase in the reversed order, they will find the expression a little odd and obviously unauthentic.

On another occasion one of the expat art directors ponders over a TV spot for a joint-venture brewery. "In North China," he asks the local staff, "what do people usually drink at a wedding banquet?" "Beer at a wedding banquet" appears to be something he is thinking about. He continues to ask, "What do people in this part of the country normally say when they invite others to come for a beer?" and "How do they say it?" A local staff member suggests to him several possible local ways of saying "come and have a beer." However, the local person feels the association between beer and wedding banquet is less than appropriate even though it is not totally culturally incorrect. Chinese do drink beer at wedding banquets, but they probably find beer more of a refreshment drink consumed in summer rather than a drink at the ritualistic wedding banquet.

With such cooperative efforts in advertising production, it is virtually impossible to assert that the production of a commercial at the Agency is genuinely local or foreign. Local production companies are often hired to produce TV commercials even though they are not equipped with the most advanced technologies and facilities. It is still more economical to produce a TV spot in China than having it done overseas. Some of these companies hire art directors from Hong Kong and Taiwan to improve their creative concepts. For the Agency, some of its TV commercials are shot locally, but post-production is done in Hong Kong, where top-of-the-line facilities are available. According to one art director at the Agency, local production companies are more experienced than overseas production teams in shooting outdoor scenes, such as the natural landscape in China. But for domestic scenes such as spots inside a house or apartment, overseas production seems more desirable. The local production companies seem to have limited direct experience with modern homes and their ambiance. This affects the interpretation and execution of ad concepts that often make use of homes as a lifestyle symbol.

The role of the local staff is equally prominent in the circulation of the finished ads. No matter how great the advertised product is and how creative its advertising message is, one needs to establish and maintain an effective circulation network to make the ad accessible to the consumer. Otherwise the advertising process remains incomplete. The advertising circulation process at the Agency involves media planning, buying, and monitoring. Facing the Agency are three key issues:

1. Mapping out the Chinese media structure
2. Selecting the media mix
3. Controlling the circulation process.

It is necessary to first assess the availability and characteristics of the mass media in China. Because of the increasing volume and variety of the Chinese media, there seems to be no shortage of media outlets for advertising campaigns. However, China's media map is vast, multi-layered, and complex, hence presenting a major challenge for ad agencies to evaluate and select the most effective and efficient media mix for their clients.

Furthermore, the uneven social and economic development (the more affluent coastal vs. the less-developed inland regions) also entails enormous disparity of media development and availability for advertising in different regions of the country. Accurate and reliable data about the cost and coverage of the media are still not available. Nowadays media outlets prepare their own media kits for ad agencies, but their figures are more often than not inflated. The woeful lack of such accurate data becomes a big challenge for the Agency to plan effective advertising.

The Agency's experience in China also demonstrates another acute problem in advertising circulation: How to ensure that the local media will live up to advertising contracts when there is no established third party monitoring mechanism in the country. Without monitoring, the media may not broadcast ads according to the contract. This is particularly a problem with local broadcast media. When neither the advertiser nor the ad agency is watching, the local TV can easily make changes in the broadcast schedule to serve their own interests. For print, the Agency always asks for a copy of the newspaper or magazine in which the ad appears. But for broadcast, self-report seems to be out of the question. The Agency needs people to tune in at particular times to check whether the commercials are on the air and to ensure that the media outlets honor the contract. The Agency has to devise its own monitoring network for ad campaigns outside major cities. Here is an example of such an endeavor at the Agency.

An ad campaign is scheduled to begin the coming weekend.

The media department is racing against the clock to deliver the tapes and ad copies to the media outlets by the deadline. There will be print, radio, and TV ads in the provincial and local media in several major cities in a neighboring province. Because of the time constraint, the media staff have to deliver, in person, finished ad copies and tapes to the designated media. The campaign is scattered around the province, so each of the media staff on this project is assigned to several media in a specific city.

One final thing before departure is to locate people who can help monitor local media. The Agency faces a formidable challenge as to how to provide monitoring service to its clients. It has tried to build up a monitoring network in the province but has not been successful in locating enough people for the current task even though it pays a handsome fee for the monitoring service provided by individuals. The media staff have been calling friends and acquaintances, looking for people they know residing in that province. The last resort is to ask the local broadcast media for names of people who may be interested. However, the Agency clearly sees a conflict of interest in having the local media recommend people who will monitor them. Moments before everyone departs, several radio and TV stations are still without designated monitoring people. Finally, out of desperation the staff decide to ask the local print media for help to find some people. Since they are not asking the broadcast media, the potential conflict of interest is minimized.

The Transfer of Professionalism

Still at its nascent stage, advertising in China has yet to carve out its own distinct identity. Many of the Chinese shops are auxiliary units to the mass media. Although advertising is now widely perceived in China as a valuable, independent service that provides value to advertisers as they compete in an increasingly more liberalized marketplace, in practice, the conduct of advertising workers seems to fall short of the professional ideal.

For instance, local account executives at the Agency often act as "messengers" rather than "facilitators" in managing agency-client relationships. In the case of being a messenger, the account executive tends to dutifully pass whatever the client wants onto the media and creative departments. "Yet what an account executive ought to be doing," explains the general manager, "is to analyze clients' requests and see if they have any merits. Often times, clients are only making offhand remarks. The account executive should present his/her views and suggestions rather than simply passing around the information." The lack of commercial concepts and experience in advertising seems to have resulted in such passivity on the part of local account executives. The management at the Agency therefore emphasizes to its local employees the value and contribution their professional service can provide to advertisers. It encourages the local staff to be more assertive on the job and to appreciate the indispensable role advertising plays in the marketplace.

Another professional norm associated with Western advertising is professional objectivity, which requires that advertising planning and execution be based on careful analyses of the market and the media rather than on mere personal opinions and preferences. The service the Agency provides to its clients is based on careful research, which follows a standard format in Western advertising of identifying marketing, communication, and creative objectives and strategies. Except for the creative side, market and media analyses, which employ such quantitative and qualitative methods as surveys and focus groups, serve as the bedrock of advertising strategy and rationale.

The selection of advertising media, for example, does not rest solely on whom one knows in a particular media organization—a prevalent practice in Chinese local advertising. Neither does the decision depend exclusively on some untested local judgment or experience. Rather, evidence from research appears to play a significant role in advertising planning. For instance, when the Agency plans and executes the advertising campaign for the product launch for an international pharmaceutical company, it identifies seven steps in the media planning for the product launch campaign. The planning starts with an understanding of the client's marketing objectives and an analysis of the competitor's media strategies. It then defines the media objectives for this campaign and develops specific media strategies. An explanation of how to execute the media buy ensues. The last two steps involve the monitoring of spot allocation and an evaluation of campaign effectiveness.

Like other businesses in China, the burgeoning Chinese advertising industry is more characterized by personal networking (guanxi) than perhaps those in a Western economy. In the absence of research and analysis, personalities and connections become decisive factors in the advertising business. But as a business and profession, advertising requires an element of rationality. In this regard the Agency's reliance on research and analysis helps to construct at least some scientific and rational foundation for the industry, and hence brings credibility to this young and unfolding trade in China.

The Agency also prides itself on upholding the integrity of the advertising business in the Chinese market. One important measure of such professionalism is that, as a company rule, the Agency's employees are strictly forbidden to receive kickbacks from media or clients in any business-related transaction. For service compensation, the Agency uses the commission system. The service fee is based on 10% to 15% of the total media billing. Sometimes the agency fee is included in the prices quoted by the media. If not included, the agency will add a flat 15% surcharge to the original total. In contrast to the local practices, the Agency's "no kickback" policy helps to make the advertising business in China more transparent and credible.

The professional objectivity and integrity embody the essence of rationality in work. Rationalization, according to Max Weber's theoretical construct, refers to "the process by which explicit, abstract, intellectually calculable rules and procedures are increasingly substituted for sentiment, tradition, and rule of thumb in all aspects of activity."[9]

To be professional is also to be perceived that way. "When we make hiring decisions," says one supervisor, "in addition to other qualifications, we also look for people who are presentable. After all, we are in the image business." Being presentable appears to largely refer to one's communication skills, both verbal and non-verbal, and appearance. Everyone at the Agency is equipped with business cards. Over the phone, the unfailingly friendliness of the Agency's staff conveys a sense of professionalism. This warmth and politeness is a far cry from the non-welcoming, sullen responses typical of Chinese state-run offices.

In short, professionalism at the Agency has at least four dimensions—autonomy, objectivity, integrity, and image. Professional autonomy calls for an affirmation of an independent identity of advertising trade. Advertising should not be viewed as superfluous and dispensable; rather it plays a central, independent role in the consumer-oriented market economy. Professional objectivity requires that advertising planning be based on research data rather than on mere personal opinions. It involves an almost standardized ritual of marketing research, which is to define and measure the market, message, and media. Professional integrity demands a level playing field in the industry and fairness and transparency in the practice of advertising. Under-the-table kickbacks are considered an impediment to the credibility of the business. Moreover, the maintenance of the professional image in the workplace showcases as well as accentuates the high caliber of professional conduct at the Agency.

Conclusion

This chapter addresses how the roles of the foreign and the local develop and are modified as a foreign ad agency recreates itself in the Chinese setting. The experience of the Agency seems to indicate that the expansion of global advertising to China is a process of reinvention that involves domestic and foreign economic and cultural practices, and cooperation and constraints.

In discussing the cross-cultural transfer of management models, Matthias Kipping and Ove Bjarnar pointed out, "Concerning the nature of the transfer and translation process, they will never be predominantly demand or supply driven, but will emerge as context-specific blends of both elements."[10] The case of the Agency is an apt example of how and to what extent a foreign organizational model is "modified and moulded into the existing institutions and traditions in the receiving countries, regions, industries and companies."[11]

The structural design of the Agency is basically reproduced in the Chinese setting. However, the Agency faces constraints from the Chinese government to share ownership with a local Chinese company. The mixture of locals and expats in the workforce constitutes an effective interpretive community of global advertising to Chinese consumers. Moreover, it is also important to note that the process of the transfer of a foreign ad agency into China is an asymmetric act since the foreign and the local do not play equal parts in the process. The organization and culture represented by the foreign agency may be appropriated to various degrees the moment it steps onto Chinese soil, but the corporate culture of the foreign partner is transferred and implanted in the Agency. The Agency has aggressively asserted its value and norm in advertising practices and has clearly established its professional authority in the fledgling yet still chaotic Chinese advertising industry.

5

"Crossing the River by Feeling the Stone": Government Regulation of Foreign Advertising

The increasingly globalized economy has revived the debate from the 1960s and 1970s on whether nation-states, under the new socio-economic context, are still capable of managing effectively their economies and societies.[1] Whether one celebrates or denigrates globalization trends, the consensus seems to be that the state's authority "has leaked away," or is giving way to the growing power of multinational corporations in people's everyday lives around the world.[2]

Although it has welcomed foreign investment, the Chinese government has not always been receptive to foreign influences and, in particular, if such influences are in the realm of culture and ideology. As argued in the previous chapters, commercial advertising represents not only a mediated economic transaction between the manufacturer and the consumer but also a cultural transaction between the ads and their target audience. Thus, advertising policy is both business and cultural policy. It is therefore not surprising that in the face of the Advertising Law of the People's Republic, the "supposedly unstoppable drumming bunny in the Duracell battery commercials came to a halt" in China because the ads violated the no superlative and comparative advertising rule. Neither was Budweiser's "King of Beers" claim found acceptable.[3]

This chapter illustrates how the Chinese government's advertising regulation applies to foreign advertising and discusses whether the globalization of economy and advertising spells the doom of the government's power to regulate and control foreign advertising content and practice.[4] (In this discussion, the concept of regulation is limited to government policies.)

Background

Since the reopening of the Chinese market and the reintroduction of commercial advertising, advertising in China has experienced three major developing phases. The first phase was between 1979 and 1983, when the Chinese government provided strong support for the reestablishment of advertising albeit there were no specific guidelines for advertising practices.[5] During the early stage of advertising development in post-Mao China, the functions and principles of advertising in a socialist system were debated in the Chinese media. The consensus appeared to be that advertising was an indispensable tool to communicate the "successes of the economic policy and the progress toward modernization."[6] In this respect, commercial advertising was close to a form of political marketing.

During the second phase (1984-1989), the Chinese government continued to promote advertising through, for example, sponsoring The Third World Advertising Congress in Beijing, June 16-20, 1987. It began to place more emphasis on regulating advertising in order to protect consumer interests and improve industry standards. But during the entire 1980s, government policies on advertising were "in a state of flux" and "not clearly defined," and the implementation and enforcement of regulations was weak.[7]

Although the economic reform was temporarily put on a hold in the aftermath of the 1989 Tiananmen incident in Beijing, the speed of reform in fact accelerated in the early 1990s, and so did the development of advertising. In 1993 the State Administration for Industry and Commerce and the State Planning Commission jointly announced an initiative for the development of the advertising industry. They laid down five basic principles. The government

1. aims to boost the Chinese advertising industry through market mechanisms.
2. emphasizes the role of the professional management of the industry.
3. wants advertising to promote Chinese culture and to contribute to China's material and spiritual civilization.
4. is keen on internationalizing the industry so that the domestic sector can learn the best practices in other countries.
5. encourages the training of advertising professionals to help improve industry practices.[8]

The 1990s marked the third period of Chinese advertising development and saw not only the rapid expansion of the industry but also the institutionalization of the first advertising law in the history of the People's Republic in 1995.

Regulating Foreign Advertising

Under the economic liberalization policies in post-Mao China, the Chinese government has strongly encouraged foreign investment in China, but as Pitman Potter observed, it also "has consistently made clear its intent to supervise foreign business activities closely."[9] The presence of foreign ad agencies in China similarly raises several key public policy issues. The concerns are primarily over the prospect of foreign domination of the advertising market and the unwanted cultural impact through advertising.[10]

China has been a favored destination of foreign investment since it reopened its doors to the West. Foreign investment enterprises have taken the basic forms of equity joint venture, contractual joint venture, and wholly foreign-owned enterprises. Equity joint ventures are business arrangements where the Chinese and foreign parties each take an equity share.[11] The managerial control in equity joint ventures is often determined by each party's capital contribution. The initial joint-venture law required that the Chinese party have at least 50% equity holding in the new entity, but that law has been relaxed.[12]

Foreign enterprises adopt the equity joint venture for several reasons. One rationale for such an arrangement is that it is required by the government as a condition of market entry. The formation of equity joint venture is also attributed to the need for the other party's skills, such as technical and managerial know-how or the knowledge of the local market. In addition, there may be a need for the assets of the other partner, such as cash, patents, and raw material sources, or for the attributes, such as the use or manufacture of certain products and services.[13] In the case of multinational ad agencies' establishing joint ventures in China, the reasons of government pressure and the need for knowledge of the local market and managerial know-how of the foreign partner appear most applicable.

The cultural function of advertising is also widely acknowledged in China as well as in the West. The economic definition of advertising as the dissemination of product information is only half of the story.[14] One key characteristic of advertising, according to one Chinese advertising handbook, is "its relatively strong ideological content. In a class society, the essence of such an ideology reflects the thoughts of the class. In order to protect the interests of a class, any government will naturally try to strengthen its management of the advertising market."[15] Title I, Article III of the Advertising Law of the PRC stipulates that "advertising should be truthful, legal and in accordance with the demands of a *socialist spiritual civilization*" (italics added). Chen Muhua, one of the senior PRC government officials and Honorary President of the China Advertising Association, stressed that advertising should be socially responsible to achieve both material and spiritual civilization.[16] As Raymond So, Chairman and CEO of J. Walter Thompson China, also pointed out, the tension in advertising regulation in China is none other than the result of "the struggle between the country's socialist ideology and its drive towards capitalism."[17]

Since the Chinese government still doesn't permit wholly foreign-owned advertising companies inside China, foreign agencies can only operate in China in the form of a joint venture, with a local Chinese partner. In 1991 the State Administration for Industry and Commerce (SAIC) spelled out conditions under which foreign investment was permitted into the Chinese advertising market. One guideline was that foreign operations should "reach scales" and introduce "advanced technologies, equipment and management experience." SAIC also required that joint-venture companies handle foreign accounts and that its equity holding not exceed 49%.[18] As in general joint-venture laws, the minority equity provision has since been relaxed. That's why many multinational ad agencies have a majority equity share in the joint venture.

To promote industry standards and consumer interests, there have been four major pieces of policy promulgated on advertising since the return of commercial advertising in post-Mao China. In 1982 the State Council issued "Provisional Regulations for Advertising Management." Then came the "Regulation for Advertising Management" of 1987, also under the auspices of the State Council. Another important advertising policy initiative was the "Interim Regulations on the Advertising Agency System" and the "Interim Advertising Review Standards" by the State Administration of Industry and Commerce in 1993. The culmination of all these efforts was the ratification of the "Advertising Law" by the National People's Congress, which came into effect in February 1995. Since the National People's Congress is the highest legislative body of the land, the Advertising Law of 1995 overrides all other previous stipulations.[19] A comparison of these documents shows that the content of advertising regulation has evolved significantly over the years. In general, it has become less ideological and more oriented toward promoting an internationally recognized standard of advertising practice, e.g., adoption of the advertising agent system.[20]

Although legal autonomy has been advocated and advanced in recent years, the Chinese legal institution is in many ways still an extension of state administration. As Stanley Lubman pointed out, "To say that [Chinese] courts are at best only co-ordinate with those other bureaucracies is only another way of expressing how far away China is from establishing a notion of the supremacy of law, at least as that concept is conceived in the West."[21] The lack of legal autonomy is largely attributed to the powerful presence of PRC government officials in various sectors of Chinese society. As Lubman observed, "A more decisive constraint on the capacity of the courts to develop either professionalism or autonomy is the continuing role of Chinese Communist Party officials, who can influence the outcome of individual cases at all levels."[22] This also applies to advertising law and regulation.

The Censorship Process

Even though the Chinese media distinguish a domestic advertising agency from a foreign agency in setting advertising rates, the Advertising Law does not create a separate category specifically for foreign advertising. "We treat local and foreign advertising equally," according to one government official. "They [foreign agencies] go through exactly the same review procedure as local advertising."[23]

In Beijing, typically, after developing a storyboard for a TV spot, the foreign advertising agency will send it to the advertising review board of the Chinese Advertising Association (CAA) for what the agency people call "censorship." Established in 1981, CAA is the national trade organization for the advertising industry. It represents ad agencies around the country and works closely with the government body (i.e., SAIC) that regulates advertising.

The CAA advertising review board interprets the nation's Advertising Law. It issues opinions about whether an ad violates or is within the confines of the law. It does not, however, have any authority to enforce laws and regulations in advertising. Although submission for review is not mandatory, it certainly is to the benefit of agencies and advertisers to do so. In most cases, once an ad passes the "censorship" at CAA, it is unlikely to be rejected by the Chinese media.

One of the sources of confusion over the legal boundaries of advertising expression is that the Advertising Law was written in broad terms and is open to various interpretations. Medical advertising, for instance, cannot be associated with the image of sick people, doctors, or other experts (Article XIV, Section IV). This is mainly to avoid misleading consumers about the efficacy of advertised medicine as doctors and experts wield tremendous authority and credibility before the public. Debatable, for instance, is what constitutes the image of a sick person. Agencies that handle medical advertising have often encountered the sick person image problem in their medical ads since the definition is not always clear and precise.

The CAA review often finds some alterations are necessary for many of the sketches or storyboards to meet the general standards set forth in the Advertising Law. After revisions are made and CAA gives approval of the revisions, the creative department of the agency enters the production stage.

Here are examples of the censorship of two television commercials (TVCs):

TVC(I).

Man 1:	What is that pain-relief medicine we had when we were abroad?
Woman:	Benix (a pseudonym). Do you have a headache?
Man 1:	No, it's for Mom.
Man 2:	Is Benix effective?
Man 1:	Would I give it to Mom if it is not effective?
Man 3:	Benix, dissolves fast and relieves your headache right away.

(On the screen: Gentle on the stomach.)

Woman:	Mom says she is going to cook some nice dishes and have us over tomorrow.
Woman:	Benix, solves all the headaches.

The storyboard of this TVC was submitted to CAA for review. CAA issued an opinion that the word "all" in the last sentence should be dropped. The Advertising Law does not permit the use of superlative words and phrases or any other unsubstantiated claims (Article VII, Section II). Alteration was done as recommended.

TVC(II).

Wife:	My husband is very demanding. For shampoo, removing dandruff only is not good enough. It should also moisturize hair.
Husband:	In the past, not only did I have dandruff but also my hair felt so dry. Thanks to my wife. She discovered Salon (a pseudonym).
Voice-over:	Introducing the new Salon, anti-dandruff treatment shampoo. It contains not only anti-dandruff formula but also Vitamin B5 which nourishes your hair.
Wife:	No dandruff. And the hair is shining.
Husband:	Only this is good enough.
Voice-over:	Salon, the anti-dandruff treatment shampoo. Dandruff disappears, and only healthy hair stays.
Husband:	I am demanding. But finally I've found it.

After reviewing the storyboard, CAA advised that the agency and the advertiser must produce laboratory certification for claiming that the shampoo was able to remove dandruff. The certification should be issued by a credible, neutral third party, preferably a government agency. Certification from an international source was also acceptable. To meet the government requirement, the agency that produced this ad provided laboratory certification by a third party.

To satisfy the requests from the authorities, one of Nike's TVCs had to edit out politically and culturally sensitive references to "no rules" and "freedom." To appease the government, a Pepsi TVC had to be modified because the actor in the Pepsi ad was shown not observing the traffic lights.[24]

The last gatekeepers in this process are the advertising media. They review all ads to be broadcast or printed. The media establish their own advertising review mechanisms. They reserve the right to reject any advertising deemed inappropriate for print or broadcast. Although many of the Chinese media are now primarily supported by advertising, they still remain in essence state-owned entities. Propaganda and profit are therefore equally important for them. Without one or the other they won't be able to survive in this new media environment. The major media are particularly stringent about advertising content because they cannot afford to bear the brunt of deviating from the government and party line.

In spring 1996, for instance, Beijing TV had set up its own guidelines for the acceptance of commercials. It required that the advertising theme adhere to the current central and municipal governments' political line. All commercials also should comply with the Advertising Law and other government regulations, and observe Chinese language standards. Moreover, ad content must not contain descriptions that promote pornography, high consumption, rock 'n' roll, and other social ideals deemed unsuitable for children. These stipulations are not really established in the codified Advertising Law, yet they are not totally incongruent with the spirit of the law either. Such measures are more politically than legally motivated. In China the political and the legal are often intricately intertwined.

With its far-reaching impact across China, China Central Television (CCTV), China's only network TV, is more cautious in observing the Advertising Law than are provincial stations. Its verdict on accepting or rejecting an ad is sometimes also a result of administrative interference from government officials and the current party line. For example, in recent years Chinese youth culture has been dazzled by entertainment celebrities from Hong Kong, Taiwan, and Western countries. To discourage teenagers from becoming preoccupied with star-chasing, CCTV takes heed of the government's concern and does not allow the identification of celebrities in the spots. Therefore, one can see two virtually identical commercials on CCTV and Beijing TV. In the former, the name of the celebrity has been withdrawn from the screen; in the latter, the star is identified by name.

The CAA review board has become such an important buffer that the major media outlets, such as China Central TV and Beijing TV, strongly recommend that ad agencies submit their ad sketches or storyboards for review at CAA. Even though CAA is not regarded as a government agency in the Chinese political structure, its approval stamp seems to carry an almost official ring.

Although sending ads to CAA for review is voluntary, it is customary for ad agencies to seek approval from CAA for their ads before production and submission to the media. In general, this process of "censorship" applies to TV ads more than to print ads. One major consideration is that by detecting potential problems at an early stage of ad production (i.e., at the storyboard stage), the agency and the advertiser can save money and effort if the ads are found to violate the Advertising Law and need to be altered.

The CAA advertising review is also a bureaucratic process. To submit for review, the agency needs to compile all the required documentation about the ad agency, the advertiser, and the advertised product. For instance, one major agency in Beijing plans an ad spot for a joint-venture beer company. In its application for review, the agency furnishes the following materials:

- Ad registration form from SAIC
- Business license of the agency
- Business license of the joint-venture beer company
- Advertising contract between the agency and the advertiser
- Detailed description of the advertising campaign
- Permit for alcohol beverage production
- Trademark registration form
- Contract between the local and foreign partners of the joint-venture brewery
- Hygiene permit from the local public health department

When the application is submitted, CAA signs an agreement with the agency that delineates both parties' rights and responsibilities in the review process. The review costs 150 yuan (a little less than US$20) per TV spot or 100 yuan per print copy for CAA members (1996 figures). Nonmembers can also use the CAA service, but the fee for review is doubled. The review board usually issues a report on the ad under consideration within three working days. After alterations are carried out according to CAA's recommendation, CAA issues an approval certificate on the final version of the spot.

All the ads submitted for CAA's review are also filed in the official record of SAIC. When the CAA review board is unsure of its interpretation of the Advertising Law, it turns to SAIC for advice.

The Power of State Regulation

One important aspect of regulation is whether the government is effective and consistent in designing and implementing the law. The "defective state" proposition contends that with the rise of a global economic infrastructure comes the decline of the role the state plays in international economic and even cultural transactions. In other words, the power of the state to oversee and manage (international) business is significantly weakened. "Collectively they [nation-states] are still the most influential and therefore critical sources of authority in the world system," argued Susan Strange, "but they are increasingly becoming hollow, or defective, institutions. To outward appearances unchanged, the inner core of their authority in society and over economic transactions within their defined territorial borders is seriously impaired."[25]

The experience of the multinational advertising industry in China seems to suggest that the Chinese government still holds enormous power in influencing and sometimes even determining foreign advertising behavior. Such government authority derives from the state and, more importantly, its legitimacy to speak on behalf of the nation and to police and regulate foreign advertising content and practice.

The impact of the 1995 Advertising Law was "immediate and

powerful" to the multinational advertising industry in China. When the law first came into effect, there was "a brief period of total confusion and frustration among agencies, particularly international agencies with multinational clients, and media controllers."[26] The confusion and frustration arise from the different interpretations of the Advertising Law. Even though foreign advertising executives complain about the vagueness and the broadness of the Advertising Law, they generally make efforts to abide by it and present the image of a good corporate citizen in China. Before the production of TV commercials, foreign agencies in Beijing dutifully submit the storyboard to CAA for review and approval. They make changes and modifications as recommended by CAA. "We just try to use our common sense in dealing with the Chinese regulations and bureaucracy," an expatriate executive at a multinational agency in Beijing remarked. "When the Advertising Law first came out, we were not familiar with its stipulations and interpretations. But now we have a much better sense of the law."[27]

Although many of the multinational advertising affiliates in China have management control over almost all aspects of the ad production process, they nevertheless face constraints from the Chinese government in designing and delivering their advertising messages to Chinese consumers. One of the suggestions made to the foreign advertising community in China is most telling of the cooperative spirit of foreign businesses when dealing with the PRC government regulation.

> Both clients and agencies should seize the opportunity to show the [PRC] government that they have actively taken the new law into consideration. Research findings could communicate to the appropriate authorities that: you respect and agree with the law; you respect the authorities; your advertisement is acceptable.[28]

The Chairman of J. Walter Thompson China simply pointed out, "You have to be flexible and prepared to change. You should also be prepared for the worst."[29]

Professionalization of Regulation

Because of the peculiar political structure, the practices of advertising regulation and self-regulation in China are one and the same. "While the reform policies enacted in 1978 permitted China to develop greater ties with the international systems of commerce and finance," Pitman Potter wrote, "state control over foreign business has remained a singular norm of the regulatory regime."[30] The Advertising Law has become the primary codified legal text for the advertising industry in China. The implementation and enforcement of the law rests within the jurisdiction of the State Administration for Industry and Commerce. It is the China Advertising Association, an industry organization, which conducts the review of advertising.

In theory, CAA's approval is not legally binding. The media also reserve their final authority to reject or accept an ad. In practice, because of the breadth of the Advertising Law and the often indeterminate interpretation of it, even the media outlets feel compelled to have some element of assurance from CAA in the form of its approval certificate. Unlike the regulatory mechanism of the advertising business in the West that takes the two basic forms of government regulation and business self-regulation, industry self-regulation in the Chinese advertising industry becomes tantamount to government regulation.

Nevertheless, advertising regulation in China is increasingly governed by a more transparent legal framework rather than being subjected to the whims of personalities. When discussing the role of the state in the evolving international political and economic environment, Vivien A. Schmidt argued,

> The unwritten story behind the internationalization of trade lies not so much in how international and regional trade associations are diminishing the autonomy of the nation-state, or in how multinationals are escaping the control of the nation-state, but in how nation-states have been altering their policies and policy-making processes to function in the new international arena.[31]

Nation-states' responses to internationalization, according to Schmidt, are not uniform. The various responses depend on factors such as the decision-making process, country size, culture, history, government structure, labor history, business size, and nature of business organization. It appears that the Chinese government has chosen to respond to the business and cultural challenges resulting from the internationalization of the advertising market by making efforts to regularize and professionalize the management and control of advertising behavior.

As are the overall Chinese legal system and culture, advertising regulation in China is characterized by a lack of autonomy of legal regime, indeterminacy in interpretation, and thus low predictability. To borrow the late Chinese leader Deng Xiaoping's much quoted phrase, the multinational ad agencies in China are also "crossing the river by feeling the stone." Nonetheless, the promulgation of the Advertising Law and other policy efforts signaled a significant step toward the rationalization and professionalization of advertising regulation in China.

6

Global Advertising, Chinese Style

Thus far we have explored and explained the content and practice of foreign advertising in China as well as the broader social, historical context in which the institution of foreign advertising has developed. In this chapter, we discuss the dialectic relationship between the global and the local as it is exemplified in this book.

Toward Cultural Hybridities

The concepts of cultural imperialism and of "*glocalization*" are two intellectual tools that one can employ to make sense of contemporary media flow across national borders. The media imperialism perspective maintains that the Western media industry is a cultural agent and that the dissemination of its products in the Third World represents cultural assault and domination. As a corollary, the expansion of Western advertising, emblematic of Western consumerism, in developing countries is also symptomatic of media imperialism. In fact, such concerns are not just confined within academic circles. Jeffrey E. Garten, Dean of the Yale School of Management, wrote in his *Business Week* column, "'Cultural imperialism' is no joke." Garten argued from the business perspective why cultural imperialism is not desirable: "Being more sensitive to foreign concerns would ease the prospect of backlash and even bolster America's ability to export its ideas and ideals for the long haul."[1]

Nevertheless, as an analytical tool, the imperialism framework has been under critical scrutiny and challenge. As Jan Nederveen Piererse pointed out,

> This is not to say that the notion of global cultural synchronization (Schiller 1989; Hamelink 1983) is irrelevant, on the contrary; but it is fundamentally incomplete. It overlooks the countercurrents—the impact non-Western cultures have been making on the West. It plays down the ambivalence of the globalizing momentum and ignores the role of the local reception of Western culture; for example, the indigenization of Western elements. It also fails to see the influence non-Western cultures have been exercising on one another. It leaves no room for cross-over cultures in the development of "Third cultures," such as world music. It overrates the homogeneity of Western culture and overlooks the fact that many of the standards exported by the West and its cultural industries themselves turn out to be of culturally mixed character if we examine their cultural lineages.[2]

The notion of globalization in both the academic and popular press typically refers to "a social process in which constraints of geography on social and cultural arrangements recede and in which people become increasingly aware that they are receding."[3] This only suggests the development of cultural convergence but slights the heterogenizing force of local cultures in the change process (e.g., George Ritzer's McDonaldization thesis[4]). The idea of "glocalization," on the other hand, takes into account both the global in the local and the local in the global. The Oxford English

Dictionary defines "global" as "pertaining to or embracing the totality of a number of items, categories, etc." and "pertaining to or involving the whole world, world-wide; universal." The term "local" refers to "belonging to a particular place on the earth's surface; pertaining to or existing in a particular region or district." In the modernist teleology, Arif Dirlik pointed out, the connotations of these two terms are strikingly opposite: the local as "enclaves of backwardness left out of progress, as the realm of rural stagnation" and the global as "dynamism of the urban, industrial civilization of capitalism" and "scientific rationality." Or, the construct of local is as a place of integration and homogeneity embodied by "myths of belonging, warmth, and togetherness" in stark contrast to the dehumanizing practices and effects of the globalizing forces.[5] These two opposing views are in fact part and parcel of each other. We can hardly speak of global without local, and vice versa.

The concept of glocalization represents the interlocking duality of globalization and localization in cultural change and formation. It is a dialectic process between universalism and particularism, and homogenization and heterogenization. The global and the local can be either the "thesis" or "antithesis," and the outcome of their relationship is the "synthesis." To borrow Benjamin Barber's description, "Jihad is not only McWorld's adversary, it is its child. The two are thus locked together in a kind of Freudian moment of the ongoing cultural struggle, neither willing to coexist with the other, neither complete without the other."[6] As Jan Nederveen Pieterse contended, such a process involves "interculturalism" rather than either "universalism" or "multiculturalism." Viewing globalization "in terms of homogenization, or of modernization/Westernization, [is] empirically narrow and historically flat."[7]

Most of the world's cultures are no longer isolated. Nor are they impervious to change. In encounters between a powerful society and a parochial one, the dominated tend to undergo changes in their social structure and cultural patterns to accommodate the directions and standards embodied and provided by the dominating. But resistance to complete capitulation to foreign cultures has also been part of the process of domination and assimilation. In some instances, conquerors opted to adopt the culture of the conquered rather than imposing their own on the conquered, as illustrated in ancient Egypt and the invasion of China by Mongolians and Manchurians.

The process of glocalization is that of hybridization, a continuum of adaptation between the global and the local. Differing conditions give rise to varying combinations of the global and the local. Although neat categories are more imaginary than real, here are, for instance, three possible scenarios of the global-local fusion. They can be located respectively on the global-local continuum.

Scenario 1, where there is strong globalization but weak localization, entails "the production of similar kinds of subjects on a global scale."[8] An example of such a situation would be the global adoption of television as a mass communication medium. There is virtually no locally significantly modified version of the television technology.

Scenario 2 represents a more balanced correspondence between global and local elements. For example, news in China tends to share the Western news emphasis on international natural disasters. But it also shows interest in Third World development news.

Scenario 3 depicts a situation where, in Friedman's words, "the local assimilates the global into its own realm of practiced meaning."[9] This can be found in the example of the prevalently local interpretation and understanding of foreign television programs.[10]

In summary, the dynamics in cultural change are perhaps as old as human society, even though the (re)discovery and the debate of theoretical conceptualization are quite recent. Perhaps what is unique in the late 20th century is that with the aid of advanced communication technology, the scope and speed of social and cultural change is unprecedented in human history, and the role of media and communication is ever more prominent and vital.

Becoming Global, Becoming Local

The case of the development of foreign advertising in China is a good illustration of the global-local logic in contemporary media contact and change. Our key concern is how advertising, a quintessentially Western institution, has been recreated in the Chinese setting and how the roles of the global and the local are negotiated in the process.

It is impossible to use a blanket statement of "globalization" or "localization" to describe foreign advertising development in China. The case, however, does suggest a coexistence of both the globalization and localization tendencies. We can grasp such a hybrid reality by disaggregating the institution of advertising into various aspects (e.g., content and practice) and identifying the differing movements of globalization and localization at various levels.

At the highest level, the fundamental concept of advertising has achieved a strong degree of globalization. As pointed out earlier, like other contemporary media technologies, advertising as a form of modern industry is a Western invention. Following the footprints of Marco Polo, legions of Western traders and missionaries arrived in China in the 19th century in search of wealth and believers. China had then been mostly a self-sufficient, enclosed society. Among the many novel ideas and practices Westerners brought with them to China were mass media and modern advertising.

Clustered in port cities like Shanghai and Hong Kong, the first major newspapers and magazines in China were predominantly owned and operated by Westerners. The *Shun Pao*, the most well-known newspaper before the period of the PRC, was founded in 1872 by an English merchant named Ernest Major and was later bought by Chinese companies. The first major advertising agencies were also established by foreigners in China. The two largest Chinese advertising companies in the 1920s and 1930s, China Commercial Advertising Agency and Consolidated National Advertising Co., were formed and managed by Chinese entrepreneurs who had received education in the United States.

The concept of modern advertising in China was an import from the West, and Western influence was critical in the introduction of modern advertising to China. In the early 20th century, advertising in China, for the most part, catered to well-to-do

Chinese and foreign communities living and working in China. The advertising business was concentrated in only a handful of cities. The 1920s and 1930s were considered the first "golden age" of advertising in modern Chinese history. As Baiyi Xu wrote,

> Historically, Western marketing techniques have proved to be not only applicable, but quite successful in China. The work of the top advertising agencies in the 1930s, for example, closely followed the American style. Consumer commodities, such as Listerine toothpaste, successfully ran the original ads, simply making ethnic alterations in the models.[11]

During the first decades of the PRC, the nature of the command economy made advertising unnecessary. The second advertising boom finally occurred in the 1980s and 1990s. One outcome of the market-oriented reform in post-Mao China was the reintroduction of advertising as an indispensable marketing tool. The rapidly growing infrastructure of the mass media also makes it possible for advertising to reach consumers throughout the country. From the 1920s to the 1990s, advertising in China has evolved from mostly elite marketing to truly mass marketing.

Since the beginning of the 19th century, with the exception of the first decades of the PRC, the basic notion of advertising in Chinese commerce has hardly been any different from that in a Western economy. Advertising, according to a Chinese definition, refers to a means to communicate to the public information about products, services or entertainment programming by the employment of print, radio, television, billboard, film, slide, window display, product display, etc.[12] The Advertising Law of 1995, which was ratified by China's National People's Congress in October 1994, defines commercial advertising as any paid advertisements by commercial producers or service providers to promote, directly or indirectly, their products and services via a certain medium or in a certain form. A comparison of the Chinese definitions with a standard definition of advertising found in a U.S. textbook (e.g., "any paid form of non-personal communication about an organization, product, service, or idea by an identified sponsor"[13]) shows that there is a basic common understanding of the role of advertising in a market economy. Despite efforts by some to articulate the concept of "socialist advertising with Chinese character," it remains at best nebulous.[14] Pronouncements by Chinese leaders and officials on advertising also point to the shared meaning of the purpose of advertising.

The notable exception was during the first decades of the PRC when advertising was rendered irrelevant in the command economic system. During those days, what little advertising left in China (there was also advertising for exporting goods) was often taken up as a tool to serve political and propaganda purposes. Commercial advertising in this sense was virtually synonymous with political marketing.

There is a social cosmology in every (communication) technology. It is important to acknowledge that media technology such as advertising is in and of itself a piece of cultural representation. It is a by-product of a specific form of economic system. In the standard imperialism criticism of Western advertising in the developing world, there is a tendency only to suspect the advertising content, while the technology of advertising is implicitly embraced. As Jeremy Tunstall keenly pointed out, a "non-American way out of the media box is difficult to discover because it is an American, or Anglo-American, built box."[15] The only way out is to invent a new box. China did try to experiment with a new box of advertising under the central command economy. But the new box was abandoned and the old one was restored when central command economy proved to be less effective than market economy in improving the people's living standard.

In short, advertising, as a form of consumer communication, has become widespread in the increasingly liberalized world's economic and cultural landscape. The American authorship of modern advertising appears less relevant. In other words, advertising has acquired a life of its own and its essence has become universal. In this sense, the purpose of advertising in the Chinese context is also a shared global one.

Another important aspect of the concept of advertising is how its professional ideals are defined. The professional ideals in foreign advertising in China also embody a strong globalization tendency. Professional ideals set the standard for the practice of the trade. The ethnographic fragments from the case study of a multinational ad agency in Beijing demonstrate the four key aspects of advertising professionalism at the Agency: objectivity, integrity, autonomy, and image. These professional ideals and practices embody the essence of rationality in work. Rationalization is particularly evident in advertising planners' reliance on research data. Rational calculability serves as the source and foundation of intellectual authority.[16]

In contrast, much of Chinese local advertising pays relatively little attention to market research and media analysis. In local advertising, media placement is largely dependent on personal relations and networks. While the Agency adopts the "open contract plus commission" compensation method, the practice of giving and receiving kickbacks is rampant in Chinese domestic advertising. In the absence of adequate marketing research and analysis, personalities and connections become decisive factors in the advertising business.

When foreign ad agencies, such as the Agency, followed their international clients to China, they clearly wanted to adhere to their Western advertising professionalism in the vibrant yet chaotic Chinese advertising market. To ensure a successful transfer of such professionalism to its China operation, the Agency recognized the importance of establishing the mechanism of control.

Institutional design is the most fundamental mechanism for the Agency to wield its influence over the work process. The Agency formed a joint venture with a local advertising company in Beijing. In China, foreign companies tend to have greater control than their equity level would suggest.[17] With majority shareholding, the Agency also has managerial control over its day-to-day operation.

The scope of control at the Agency encompasses all of its managerial positions. The Agency, like any other full-service agency, has departments of account service, media, creative, and administrative support. The functions of these departments are similar to those in agencies in the United States. The general manager and the heads of the departments at the Agency are all expatriates.

Moreover, the division of labor among the account service, media, and creative departments at the Agency appears to reflect a basic global structural design of full-service ad agencies. Historically, ad agencies in China had also borrowed this Western structural model.[18] The departments might be called different names in different times and places but serve comparable functions in the process of ad making.

Aside from the basic concept of advertising, advertising professionalism, and institutional design, the advertising appeals of consumerism also echo the global emphasis on material pleasures and modernity. The execution tactics often take into account the Chinese cultural context, but the consumerist ethos expressed and communicated in foreign ads in China are pervasive.

For example, here is a TV ad for Pantene shampoo:

> The commercial opens with a close-up shot of the beautiful hair of a former Miss Hong Kong-turned-actress. She starts to talk to the camera, "Do you think shining hair like mine only appears on TV?" (A medium shot of her cuts in during the middle of her talk.) She is then seen walking in a room as she speaks. Then a close-up shot shows the actress talking directly to the camera, "No." She sits on a couch, touching her beautiful long hair, "You can have it too if your hair is healthy."
>
> The actress tries to comb her long hair with her hands but cannot do it. She looks a bit worried, "My hair used to be so dry until I started to use Pantene (a close-up shot of her healthy hair)." A male voice-over announces with the product shot, "Pantene, special treatment shampoo contains vitamin B5 that can penetrate your hair thoroughly (animation demo of vitamin penetration into the hair)." The male voice-over continues, "Providing nourishment and making hair healthy and shine."

> The camera turns to the long hair from the back of the actress. (A close-up shot of her face and hair.) "If there is a contest for beautiful hair," she talks to the camera, "I'll have the confidence to win again." (A shot of a series of Pantene products on display.) The male voice-over, "Pantene. Hair so healthy, it shines." A close-up back shot captures the actress turning around and talking directly to the camera again, "Try it. You can have healthy shining hair too." The commercial ends with the P&G logo.

In this commercial, the beautiful actress tries to convince consumers that clean and shining hair is a desired goal for our daily existence. When she is describing how dry her hair was before using Pantene, there is a certain anxiety on her face. This quick comparison establishes an association between unclean, dry hair and unattractiveness. Carl Crow made a keen observation more than half a century ago about the meaning of cleanliness in China, "For cleanliness everywhere is costly and when expressed in terms of other things, it is probably more expensive in China than in any other country."[19] The observation still holds true today. By Chinese standards, foreign brand name shampoos are a luxury item. However, with increasing disposable income, Chinese consumers are persuaded to seek life's pleasures in cleanliness and to put on a confident new look.

Despite the developments of convergence in advertising content and practice, advertising circulation (media planning, buying, and monitoring) are still highly localized activities. Localization is also manifest in advertising regulation/self-regulation and consumers' understanding of ads. Research has shown that media buying still remains a primarily local activity. As Sandra E. Moriarty and Thomas R. Duncan pointed out, it is not yet possible to permit a centralized global media buy because of the tremendous across-country media and cultural differences.[20]

Historically, foreign advertising also embraced a localized approach in circulating ads. For instance, in its advertising campaigns in China in the early 20th century, the British-American Tobacco Company (BAT) chose not only media that it had normally used in the West, such as newspapers, sign boards, wall paintings, etc., but also more country-specific vehicles, such as "scrolls, handbills, calendars, wall hangings, window displays, attractive and strong cigarette packing cases (whose wood and nails were reused by the Chinese), cotton canvas covers for the tops of carts, and small rugs to serve as footrests in rickshas—all bearing BAT's trademark."[21]

Cultural hybridities are conceived as a continuum. In between strong globalization and strong localization are practices that embody moderately globalized and localized. For example, the plurality of workforce and the cooperative nature of advertising production are two aspects of the foreign advertising industry in China that significantly involve both the global and the local.

From a historical standpoint, foreign advertising's reliance on local knowledge and expertise to reach the Chinese market is nothing new or unusual. One of the big foreign advertisers in China in the early part of the 20th century was BAT.

> To design appealing advertisements, BAT quickly learned to rely on Chinese who had a knowledge of Chinese traditions, an awareness of local customs, and a sensitivity to the popular imagination's cultural sensibility which Americans and other Westerners on the staff simply did not possess.[22]

In 1983, Theodore Levitt of Harvard Business School proclaimed the coming of the globalization of markets. He asserted, "The modern global corporation contrasts powerfully with the aging multinational corporation. Instead of adapting to superficial and even entrenched differences within and between nations, it will seek sensibly to force suitable standardized products and practices on the entire globe."[23] The implication of this proposition for commercial advertising is the prospect of a globally integrated, standardized advertising campaign. Levitt's argument has since generated much debate in the business and academic communities. In their article titled "The Myth of Globalization,"

Susan P. Douglas and Yoram Wind outlined formidable barriers to the marketing of standardized products around the world.[24]

From studies of foreign advertising in China, globalization of advertising is neither fully reality nor fully myth; rather, it is in many ways both. The presence and development of foreign advertising in China suggests how both globalized and localized realities in advertising practice and message intertwine during the process, thus constructing a hybrid cultural space that is simultaneously foreign and local. As Anthony Giddens has observed, globalization is "more than the diffusion of Western institutions across the world, in which other cultures are crushed. Globalization—which is a process of uneven development that fragments as it coordinates—introduces new forms of world interdependence, in which once again, there are no 'others.'"[25]

Role of Foreign Advertising in China

The foreign advertising industry introduced the practice and institution of modern advertising to China. It has helped to shape the meaning of a good life and to make it visible to Chinese consumers. The role of foreign advertising in the cultural canonization of consumerism is direct and decisive. In particular, the second coming of foreign advertising since the institutionalization of economic reform in the late 1970s has signaled the historical reversal of the hyper-politicization of communist ideology during the first decades of the PRC. As a reaction to hyper-politicization, consumer culture in China is not an ugly word. Material consumption provides a space for people to escape from the straightjacket of political ideology. There is a certain element of openness and democracy in advertising.[26] It allows goods and services to be made pubic and visible. Furthermore, the "Democracy of Goods" concept discussed by Roland Marchand also asserts that the acquisition of goods would also provide pleasure and satisfaction even though one is not rich, fortunate and famous.[27]

However, a cautionary note is necessary here. As it has been manifested in developed economies, the excess of consumer culture can also take a toll in almost the same way as the extreme political control China experienced during the pre-reform years. Only this time, it is not the dictatorship of politics but the tyranny of business. As economics assumes growing power, advertising and foreign advertising, for that matter, might exercise more control over cultural expression in China.[28]

Foreign advertising is also but one of the many indicators of the influx of foreign (Western) cultural products in China. For instance, foreign TV programs have expanded their share in the Chinese TV menu.[29] Chinese editions of Western magazines have been launched. Hollywood blockbuster movies are also released in Chinese cities. The influx of foreign advertising should not be viewed in isolation from the concomitant importation of a wide range of foreign media products in China. Foreign advertising is one component of the "cultural mix" that first reached China at the turn of the 20th century and then returned in the 1980s and 1990s.

Moreover, while the rest of the world shows great concern over the numbing effect of commercial advertising and decries its flagrant propagation of consumerist ideology, the Chinese appear to admire the Western subtle style of advertising and embrace the sophisticated advertising techniques practiced by foreign agencies.[30] Foreign ads are generally better received than domestic ads.

In short, foreign advertising defines the standard of ad quality for not only Chinese consumers but also Chinese advertising professionals. It therefore teaches styles and techniques as well as serves to orient consumption behavior. It will be interesting to find out to what extent the local Chinese advertising industry, as it grows, will absorb, adapt, or reject Western advertising practices and content, and whether a characteristically Chinese approach to advertising will evolve.[31]

Epilogue

The Cola Wars between archrivals Coke and Pepsi continue to rage on across the vast Chinese mainland. Although Coke has long established itself as a solid leader in China's fast-growing soft-drink market, challenger Pepsi appears to be gaining ground, holding a strong position in the capital city Beijing and in the economic powerhouse Shanghai. The company's aggressive tactics include advertisements featuring today's hottest pop stars, from Hong Kong canto-pop performers Faye Wang and Aaron Kwok to Western superstars Janet Jackson and Ricky Martin.[1]

Since the reform movement in the late 1970s, a consumer revolution has taken place in China. According to one projection, by 2000, 260 million people (about one-fifth of the Chinese population) will cross the income threshold for packaged goods and will be able to afford mass consumer goods.[2] If compared to the U.S. consumer market of 240 million people in 2000, the Chinese market is no doubt most significant for global consumer manufacturers as well as advertising agencies.

In the early 1980s when China was reopened to foreign advertising, the Chinese advertising market was viewed as "not forthcoming enough to justify a great deal of activity, but too important to ignore completely."[3] A decade later the surge of foreign ad agencies in China finally occurred. Today most international agencies have a well-established presence inside the country and have been building the advertising infrastructure for their long-term growth.

The clientele base of the multinational agencies remains predominantly foreign/joint-venture companies, with only 10% local clients.[4] However, there is a growing trend of Chinese companies turning to multinational agencies for the quality service, expertise, and high level of professionalism they embody. These savvy local companies and the Chinese government are increasingly keen to establish strong national or even global brands and build pillar industries in China. One of the leading Chinese consumer goods manufacturers, Haier, has in fact overtaken Proctor & Gamble as the biggest advertiser in China.[5] Within a few years' time, it would not be surprising to find brand name products from China in the global marketplace. The opportunities for multinational agencies to help establish and grow with these brands for both the local and global markets are ever more promising.

It seems clear that as multinational agencies become more global, they are also becoming more local. These agencies are facing increasingly sophisticated consumers on the mainland. Localization happens not only within the creative process of adapting advertisements and creating local messages but also within the personnel process of staffing and management. Multinational agencies also must build the capability to cultivate Chinese local clients as well as continue to provide quality service to multinational clients. As C.K. Prahalad and Kenneth Liberthal observed, "Many corporations, [however], are beginning to see that the opportunity that big emerging markets represent demands a new way of thinking. Success will require more than simply developing cultural sensitivity. The more we understand the nature of these markets, the more we believe that multinational companies will have to rethink and reconfigure every element of their business models."[6]

Advertising business is also affected by shifts, however subtle or dramatic, in the general social, economic, and political climate of a country. Amidst the regional economic depression in Asia during 1997 and 1998, the growth of advertising slackened considerably. Encouragingly, in 1999 as economic and banking reforms began to have some effect in the region, the outlook for an eventual recovery looked promising and the advertising industry too seemed to have weathered the worst of the storm. In the political arena, the 1999 NATO conflict in Yugoslavia resulted in one of the worst downturns in U.S.-China relations in years. The bombing of the Chinese embassy in Belgrade by American warplanes rekindled fervent Chinese nationalism. Ads for American products were pulled off the air in major cities as the Chinese government launched a media campaign to denounce the United States. "I personally believe," said J. Walter Thompson's Shanghai managing director Tom Doctoroff, "the potential for long-term damage to the advertising industry, particularly foreign interests, does exist."[7] On a more general level, U.S. foreign policy towards China and American business interest in China are often marred by inconsistency and conflict, which "magnifies the risks for U.S. companies in China."[8] Advertising being one of the most visible symbols of products and services and, to a greater extent, culture, its viability and development is susceptible to the swings of the public mood and opinion.

❖ ❖ ❖

The development of foreign advertising is not qualitatively new in China. The emergence of advertising during the 1920s and 1930s now seems a distant past. For foreign ad agencies, that was a prosperous era. As Carl Crow wrote,

> The possibilities of a huge and profitable trade in China had intrigued American and other manufacturers for several generations but their hopes had never been fully realized. The period of Manchu rule was one of stagnation and of opposition to all foreign ideas and the use of foreign goods. The Revolution of 1911 and the establishment of the republic appeared to promise better things. Many times during the quarter of a century following this event we thought we saw prosperity just around the corner. We never turned the corner because a civil war or some political upheaval of one sort or another always intervened. I know that so far as I was personally concerned, every time I started to make a little money it appeared to be the sig-

> nal for a Chinese warlord to ravage some part of the country, and start my Chinese accountants dipping their pens in the red-ink bottle. That had been the experience of all of my friends. But now the corner had definitely been turned. It was the opinion of all of us that there was a long period of prosperity ahead of us.[9]

On the morning of August 14, 1937, Carl Crow went to work at his agency in Shanghai. He was in a cheerful mood because his business had been going well. He sat in his office writing a letter to a U.S. toothpaste company suggesting an increase in ad spending in the following year.

> I was finishing the final draft of the letter when the window panes in my office rattled and some of them broke, from the concussion of a huge bomb which Chinese aviators had dropped in an attempt to hit the Japanese flagship anchored about two hundred yards from the desk at which I was sitting. In quick succession we heard the deafening roar of two other bombs and then the vicious staccato of anti-aircraft guns.
>
> It was in this way that the undeclared war came to me—as it came to thousands of other foreigners and to millions of Chinese who live in the colorful city of Shanghai. It marked the end of an era.[10]

As the Sino-Japanese War broke out, Westerners started to leave Shanghai for safer havens. The curtain came down abruptly on the first golden age of advertising in China.

More than 50 years have elapsed. China's second advertising boom is now well under way.

Notes

Chapter 1

1. Michael Schudson, *Advertising, The Uneasy Persuasion: Its Dubious Impact on American Society* (New York: Basic Books, 1984), p. 218.
2. *See* "The Stateless Corporation," *Business Week*, 14 May 1990, pp. 52-59; Kenichi Ohmae, "Beyond Friction to Facts: The Borderless Economy," *New Perspectives Quarterly*, Spring 1990, pp. 20-21.
3. Lester G. Thurow, *The Future of Capitalism: How Today's Economic Forces Shape Tomorrow's World* (New York: William Morrow and Company, 1996), p. 115.
4. Kwangmi K. Kim, "Spreading the Net: The Consolidation Process of Large Transnational Advertising Agencies in the 1980s and Early 1990s," *International Journal of Advertising* 14 (1995), p. 209.
5. *Advertising Age*, 15 April 1995, p. s15.
6. Armand Mattelart, *Advertising International: The Privatization of Public Sphere* (London: Routledge, 1991), p. ix.
7. *The Economist*, 12-18 October 1996, pp. 35-36.
8. *See* Russell W. Belk and Nan Zhou, "Learning to Want Things," in M. Wallendorf and P. Anderson (eds.), *Advances in Consumer Research* 14 (Provo, Utah: Association for Consumer Research, 1986), pp. 478-481; Zhao Bin and Graham Murdock, "Young Pioneers: Children and the Making of Chinese Consumerism," *Cultural Studies* 10, no. 2 (1996), pp. 201-217.
9. Orville Schell, *To Get Rich Is Glorious: China in the Eighties* (New York: Pantheon Books, 1984), p. 203.
10. *The Economist*, 3 December 1994, p. 75.
11. *The New York Times*, 25 October 1995, p. C6.
12. *The New York Times*, 6 February 1995, p. A1.

13. *Business Week*, 24 June 1996, p. 54.
14. *The New York Times*, 19 June 1996, p. C1.
15. *Reuters Business Report*, 8 October 1996.
16. *The People's Daily*, overseas edition, 17 July 1996, p. 2.
17. "Global Adspend Trends," *International Journal of Advertising* 17 (1998), pp. 255-262.
18. At the time of the study, non-Chinese ad agencies were mostly responsible for producing and disseminating ads for global consumer products. In the study, the general term "foreign advertising" is used to refer to the production and circulation of these ads.
19. Scott D. Seligman, "China's Fledgling Advertising Industry: The Start of Something Big?" *The China Business Review*, January/February 1984, p. 17.
20. *China Advertising* (in Chinese), January 1998, p. 14.
21. *China Advertising Yearbook 1996* (in Chinese) (Beijing: Xin Hua Press, 1997), p. 33.
22. *International Advertising* (in Chinese), September 1997, p. 14.
23. *Media*, Chinese edition, September/October 1998, p. 1.
24. Baiyi Xu, "The Role of Advertising in China," *Working Paper #24*, Department of Advertising, College of Communication, University of Illinois—Champaign-Urbana, U.S.A., 1989, p. 25.
25. Baiyi Xu, "Reaching the Chinese Consumer," *The China Business Review*, November/December 1992, p. 42.
26. Dong Li and Alec. M. Gallup, "In Search of the Chinese Consumer," *The China Business Review*, September/October 1995, pp. 19-22; DDB Needham, *China Bulletin*, no. 2 (September 1995).
27. Mary Douglas and Baron Isherwood, *The World of Goods* (New York: Basic Books, 1979), p. 59.
28. Robert Bocock, *Key Ideas: Consumption* (London: Routledge, 1993), p. 52.
29. James B. Twitchell, *Adcult USA: The Triumph of Advertising in American Culture* (New York: Columbia University Press, 1996), p. 4.
30. Michael Schudson, *Advertising, The Uneasy Persuasion: Its Dubious Impact on American Society* (New York: Basic Books, 1984), p. 233.
31. Erving Goffman, *Gendered Advertisements* (Cambridge, Mass.: Harvard University Press, 1979).
32. Raymond Williams, "Advertising: The Magic System," in *Problems in Materialism and Culture* (London: Verso, 1980), p. 184.

33. Stuart Ewen, *Captains of Consciousness: Advertising and the Social Roots of the Consumer Culture* (New York: McGraw-Hill Book Company, 1976), p. 109.
34. *See* Stuart Ewen, *Captains of Consciousness: Advertising and the Social Roots of the Consumer Culture* (New York: McGraw-Hill Book Company, 1976); C. Wright Mills, "The Cultural Apparatus," in *Power, Politics and People* (New York: Oxford University Press, 1963), pp. 405-422.
35. *Advertising Age International*, 15 January 1979, p. s2.
36. Ralph M. Hower, *The Story of an Advertising Agency: N.W. Ayer & Son at Work* (Cambridge, Mass.: Harvard University Press, 1939), p. 3.
37. *See*, for instance, Cees J. Hamelink, *Cultural Autonomy in Global Communication: Planning National Information Policy* (New York: Longman, 1983).

    Most of the media imperialism literature appeared in the 1970s and the early 1980s, e.g., Herbert I. Schiller, *Mass Communication and American Empire* (New York: Augustus M. Kelley Publishers, 1969); Jeremy Tunstall, *The Media Are American* (New York: Columbia University Press, 1977); International Commission for the Study of Communication Problems (The MacBride Report), *Many Voices, One World: Towards a New More Just and More Efficient World Information and Communication Order* (UNESCO, 1980); Chin-chuan Lee, *Media Imperialism Reconsidered: The Homogenizing of Television Culture* (Beverly Hills: Sage Publications, 1980).

    Scholarly interest in the debate re-emerged in the 1990s when cultural and media globalization seemed to accelerate, e.g., Herbert I. Schiller, "Not Yet the Post-imperialist Era," *Critical Studies in Mass Communication* 8 (1991), pp. 13-28; John Tomlinson, *Cultural Imperialism: A Critical Introduction*, 2nd ed. (Baltimore: The Johns Hopkins University Press, 1992); James Petras, "Cultural Imperialism in the Late 20th Century," *Journal of Contemporary Asia* 23, no. 2 (1993), pp. 139-148.
38. *See* Michael Anderson, *Madison Avenue in Asia: Politics and Transnational Advertising* (London: Associated University Presses, 1984); Herbert I. Schiller, "Madison Avenue Imperialism," in *Communication in International Politics*, ed. Richard L. Merritt (Urbana, Ill.: University of Illinois Press, 1972), pp. 318-338. *See also*

Richard J. Barnet and John Cavanagh, *The Global Dreams: Imperial Corporations and the New World Order* (New York: Touchstone, 1994).

39. *See*, for instance, Daniel Lerner, *The Passing of Traditional Society* (New York: Macmillan, 1958); Wilbur Schramm, *Mass Media and National Development* (Stanford, Calif.: Stanford University Press, 1964).
40. Herbert I. Schiller, *Mass Communication and American Empire* (New York: Augustus M. Kelley Publishers, 1969).
41. Muhammadi Ayish, "International Communication in the 1990s: Implications for the Third World," *International Affairs* 68, no. 3 (1992), p. 488.
42. Herbert I. Schiller, "Not Yet the Post-imperialist Era," *Critical Studies in Mass Communication* 8 (1991), pp. 13-28.
43. James Petras, "Cultural Imperialism in the Late 20th Century," *Journal of Contemporary Asia* 23, no. 2 (1993), p. 140.
44. *See* Michael Anderson, *Madison Avenue in Asia: Politics and Transnational Advertising* (London: Associated University Presses, 1984); Herbert I. Schiller, "Madison Avenue Imperialism," in *Communication in International Politics*, ed. Richard L. Merritt (Urbana, Ill.: University of Illinois Press, 1972), pp. 318-338.
45. For studies on South and Southeast Asia, *see*, for example, Michael Anderson, *Madison Avenue in Asia: Politics and Transnational Advertising* (London: Associated University Presses, 1984); Katherine T. Frith and Michael Frith, "Advertising as Cultural Invasion," *Media Asia* 16, no. 4 (1989), pp. 179-184, 214, and "Western Advertising and Eastern Culture: The Confrontation in Southeast Asia," *Current Issues and Research in Advertising* 12, no. 1 (1990), pp. 63-73; Kwangmi K. Kim and Katherine Frith, "An Analysis of the Growth of Transnational Advertising in Five Asian Countries: 1970-1990," *Media Asia* 20, no. 1 (1993), pp. 45-53, 56; Subir Sengupta and Katherine Frith, "Multinational Corporation Advertising and Cultural Imperialism: A Content Analysis of Indian Television Commercials," *Asian Journal of Communication* 7, no. 1 (1997), pp. 1-18.

For studies on Latin America, *see* Armand Mattelart, *Multinational Corporations and the Control of Culture: The Ideological Apparatus of Imperialism* (Atlantic Highlands, N.J.: Humanities Press, 1979); Fred Fejes, "The Growth of Multinational Advertising

Agencies in Latin America," *Journal of Communication* 30, no. 3 (1980), pp. 36-49; Noreene Z. Janus, "Advertising and the Mass Media: Transnational Link Between Production and Consumption," *Media Culture and Society* 3 (1981), pp. 13-23 and "Advertising and the Mass Media in the Era of the Global Corporation," in *Communication and Social Structure: Critical Studies in Mass Media Research*, ed. Emile G. McAnany, Jorge Schritman, and Noreene Z. Janus (New York: Praegers, 1981), pp. 287-316.

46. *See also* Kwangmi K. Kim and Katherine Frith, "An Analysis of the Growth of Transnational Advertising in Five Asian Countries: 1970-1990," *Media Asia* 20, no. 1 (1993), pp. 45-53, 56.

    For export of Western advertising and its professionalism *see,* for instance, Michael Anderson, *Madison Avenue in Asia: Politics and Transnational Advertising* (London: Associated University Presses, 1984); Katherine T. Frith and Michael Frith, "Advertising as Cultural Invasion," *Media Asia* 16, no. 4 (1989), pp. 179-184, 214.

    For transnationalization of consumer culture, *see* Noreene Z. Janus, "Advertising and the Mass Media: Transnational Link Between Production and Consumption," *Media Culture and Society* 3 (1981), pp. 13-23; Cees J. Hamelink, *Cultural Autonomy in Global Communication: Planning National Information Policy* (New York: Longman Inc., 1983).

    For commercialization of local mass media, *see* Fred Fejes, "The Growth of Multinational Advertising Agencies in Latin America," *Journal of Communication* 30, no. 3 (1980), pp. 36-49.

47. Charles F. Frazer, "Issues and Evidence in International Advertising," *Current Issues and Research in Advertising* 12, no. 1 (1990), pp. 75-90.
48. Frederick Buell, *National Culture and the New Global System* (Baltimore: The Johns Hopkins University Press, 1993), p. 5.
49. Jan Nederveen Pieterse, "Globalization as Hybridization," in *Global Modernities*, ed. Mike Featherstone, Scott Lash, and Roland Robertson (Thousand Oaks, Calif.: Sage Publications, 1995), p. 63.
50. Lawrence W. Levine, *The Opening of the American Mind: Canons, Cultures and History* (Boston: Beacon Press, 1996), p. 160.
51. Roland Robertson, "Glocalization: Time-space and Homogeneity-heterogeneity," in *Global Modernities*, ed. Mike Featherstone, Scott Lash, and Roland Robertson (Thousand Oaks, Calif.: Sage Publications, 1995), p. 27.

52. Jonathan Friedman, "Being in the World: Globalization and Localization," *Theory, Culture and Society* 7 (1990), p. 311.
53. Roland Robertson, "Glocalization: Time-space and Homogeneity-heterogeneity," in *Global Modernities*, ed. Mike Featherstone, Scott Lash and Roland Robertson (Thousand Oaks, Calif.: Sage Publications, 1995), p. 35.
54. Mike Featherstone, "Localism, Globalism, and Cultural Identity," in *Global/Local: Cultural Production and the Transnational Imaginary*, ed. Rob Wilson and Wimal Dissanayake (Durham, N.C.: Duke University Press, 1996) p. 47.
55. Anthony Giddens, *The Consequences of Modernity* (Stanford, Calif.: Stanford University Press, 1990), p. 64.
56. Robert Young, *Colonial Desires: Hybridity in Theory, Culture and Race* (London: Routledge, 1995), p. 6.
57. Ibid., p. 26.
58. Ithiel de Sola Pool, "The Changing Flow of Television," *Journal of Communication* 27 (1977), p. 145.
59. Anthony Giddens, *The Consequences of Modernity* (Stanford, Calif.: Stanford University Press, 1990), pp. 79-80.
60. John B. Thompson, *The Media and Modernity: A Social Theory of the Media* (Stanford, Calif.: Stanford University Press, 1995), p. 192.
61. Edward Said, *Culture and Imperialism* (New York: Vintage Books, 1993), p. 317.
62. Xiaomei Chen, *Occidentalism: A Theory of Counter-Discourse in Post-Mao China* (New York: Oxford University Press, 1995), pp. 15-16.
63. Jan Nederveen Pieterse, "Globalization as Hybridization," in *Global Modernities*, ed. Mike Featherstone, Scott Lash, and Roland Robertson (Thousand Oaks, Calif.: Sage Publications, 1995), p. 56.
64. Arjun Appadurai, "Disjuncture and Difference in the Global Cultural Economy," *Theory, Culture and Society* 7 (1990), p. 295.
65. Roland Robertson, "Glocalization: Time-space and Homogeneity-heterogeneity," in *Global Modernities*, ed. Mike Featherstone, Scott Lash and Roland Robertson (Thousand Oaks, Calif.: Sage Publications, 1995), p. 27.
66. Jeremy Tunstall, *The Advertising Man* (London: Chapman and Hall Ltd., 1964), p. 35.
67. Robert Young, *Colonial Desires: Hybridity in Theory, Culture and Race* (London: Routledge, 1995), p. 5.

Chapter 2

1. Raymond Williams, *Problems in Materialism and Culture* (London: Verso, 1980), p. 180.
2. Daniel Pope, *The Making of Modern Advertising* (New York: Basic Books, 1983), p. 3.
3. *See* Stuart Ewen, *Captains of Consciousness: Advertising and the Social Roots of the Consumer Culture* (New York: McGraw-Hill Books Company, 1976).
4. John K. Fairbank, *The United States and China*, 4th ed. (Cambridge, Mass.: Harvard University Press, 1979), p. 147.
5. Ibid., p. 155.
6. *See The History of the Development of Chinese Domestic Commerce and Industry* (in Chinese) (Heibei People's Press, 1997), p. 255. For detailed accounts of foreign economic activities in China in the first half of the 20th century, *see* Robert Dernberger, "The Role of Foreigner in China's Economic Development, 1840-1949," in *China's Modern Economy in Historical Perspective*, ed. Dwight H. Perkins (Stanford, Calif.: Stanford University Press, 1975), pp. 19-47; Albert Feuerwerker, *The Foreign Establishment in China in the Early Twentieth Century* (Ann Arbor: Center for Chinese Studies at the University of Michigan, 1976); Albert Feuerwerker, *The Chinese Economy, 1870-1949* (Ann Arbor: Center for Chinese Studies at the University of Michigan, 1995); Chi-ming Hou, *Foreign Investment and Economic Development in China, 1840-1937* (Cambridge, Mass.: Harvard University Press, 1965).
7. Jonathan D. Spence, *The Search for Modern China* (New York: W.W. Norton and Company, 1990), p. 329.
8. *The History of the Development of Chinese Domestic Commerce and Industry* (in Chinese) (Heibei People's Press, 1997), p. 76.
9. Michel Chossudovsky, *Towards Capitalist Restoration? Chinese Socialism after Mao* (Basingstoke, England: Macmillan Education Ltd., 1986), p. 135.
10. *The History of the Development of Chinese Domestic Commerce and Industry* (in Chinese) (Heibei People's Press, 1997), p. 72.
11. Jonathan D. Spence, *The Search for Modern China* (New York: W.W. Norton and Company, 1990), p. 329.
12. "Note on Chinese Serial," December 1854, in *Collection of Writings on Chinese Journalism History* (in Chinese), ed. Fu Dan University Department of Journalism (Shanghai: Shanghai People's Press, 1987), pp. 6-7.

13. Pei-ai Chen, *The History of Chinese and Foreign Advertising* (in Chinese) (Beijing: China Wu Jia Press, 1997), p. 38.
14. Baiyi Xu, *Marketing to China: One Billion New Customers* (Lincolnwood, Ill.: NTC Business Books, 1990), p. xxi.
15. Gongzhen Ge, *The History of Chinese Newspapers* (in Chinese) (Hong Kong: Taiping Press, 1964), p. 217.
16. *Newspaper Directory of China* (Shanghai: Carl Crow, Inc., 1937), p. IV.
17. *Newspaper Directory of China* (Shanghai: Carl Crow, Inc., 1937). For further discussion of foreign publications in China, *see* Albert Feuerwerker, *The Foreign Establishment in China in the Early Twentieth Century* (Ann Arbor: Center for Chinese Studies at the University of Michigan, 1976), p. 8.
18. *Newspaper Directory of China* (Shanghai: Carl Crow, Inc., 1937), p. VIII.
19. *Advertising and Marketing in China: Past, Present and Future* (Hong Kong: The Asia Letter, 1985), p. 154.
20. *Newspaper Directory of China* (Shanghai: Carl Crow, Inc., 1937), p. 134.
21. Interview with Baiyi Xu, Shanghai, 1996.
22. *Newspaper Directory of China* (Shanghai: Carl Crow, Inc., 1937), p. 128.
23. "China's Progress in Advertising in the Last Ten Years," originally published in 1936, reprinted in *Advertising and Marketing in China: Past, Present and Future* (Hong Kong: The Asia Letter, 1985), p. 138.
24. Andrew Nathan, *Chinese Democracy* (New York: Knopf, 1985), p. 157.
25. Baiyi Xu, *Marketing to China: One Billion New Customers* (Lincolnwood, Ill.: NTC Business Books, 1990), p. xxii.
26. *Advertising and Marketing in China: Past, Present and Future* (Hong Kong: The Asia Letter, 1985), p. 136.
27. *Newspaper Directory of China* (Shanghai: Carl Crow, Inc., 1937), p. 158.
28. Shangda Su, *Introduction to Advertising* (in Chinese) (Shanghai: The Commercial Press, 1931), pp. 5-6.
29. *All About Shanghai: A Standard Guidebook* (Hong Kong: Oxford University Press, 1986), p. 84.
30. Carl Crow, *Newspaper Directory of China* (Shanghai: Carl Crow, Inc., 1937), p. 9.

31. Tianquan Shi, *Introduction to Radio and TV* (in Chinese) (Shanghai: Fu Dan University Press, 1991), p. 12.
32. Andrew Nathan, *Chinese Democracy* (New York: Knopf, 1985), p. 158.
33. Aside from the commercial media, there were press and radio operated by, for instance, the Communist Party during those years. But they were of small circulation or restricted to certain regions. It was primarily the commercial media that furnished the ground for the rise of commercial advertising.
34. Baiyi Xu, *Marketing to China: One Billion New Customers* (Lincolnwood, Ill.: NTC Business Books, 1990), p. xxi.
35. Shanghai Academy of Social Sciences, *Shanghai Economy, 1949-1982* (in Chinese) (Shanghai: Shanghai People's Press, 1983), p. 622.
36. Baiyi Xu, "The Development of Advertising in Old Shanghai," in *Advertisements in the Old Time Shanghai* (in Chinese) (Shanghai: Shanghai Pictorial Press, 1995), pp. 3-12.
37. Shanghai Academy of Social Sciences, *Shanghai Economy, 1949-1982* (in Chinese) (Shanghai: Shanghai People's Press, 1983), p. 623.
38. Interview with Baiyi Xu, Shanghai, 1996.
39. Carl Crow, *Four Hundred Million Customers: The Friendly Chinaman and His Business* (New York: Harpers and Brothers, 1937).
40. Ibid., p. 32.
41. Ibid., p. 41.
42. Ibid., p. 217.
43. Ibid., p. 220.
44. Ibid., p. 210.
45. *Newspaper Directory of China* (Shanghai: Carl Crow, Inc., 1937), p. II.
46. There might still have been some foreign agencies operating in China during and after the Sino-Japanese War. Carl Crow wrote, "Even during the days when Shanghai was surrounded by war and every street was full of refugees and wounded were being brought in by the truck load and the air was full of the foul odor of war, advertising continued to be an essential cog in the wheel" (Crow manuscript titled "Advertising meets war and survives," p. 6, Carl Crow papers [f-29], Western Historical Manuscript Collection, Columbia, Missouri). Crow eventually left Shanghai. More research is needed to find out about the advertising business during the war.

47. "China's progress in advertising in the last ten years," originally published in 1936, reprinted in *Advertising and Marketing in China: Past, Present and Future* (Hong Kong: The Asia Letter, 1985), pp. 125, 149-153.
48. Interview with Baiyi Xu, Shanghai, 1996.
49. Gongzhen Ge, *The History of Chinese Newspapers* (in Chinese) (Hong Kong: Taiping Press, 1964), pp. 216-217.
50. *Newspaper Directory of China* (Shanghai: Carl Crow, Inc., 1937), p. IV.
51. Carl Crow, *Foreign Devils in the Flowery Kingdom* (New York: Harpers and Brothers, 1940), pp. 48-49.
52. Sherman Cochran, *Big Business in China: Sino-Foreign Rivalry in the Cigarette Industry, 1890-1930* (Cambridge, Mass.: Harvard University Press, 1980).
53. Pei-ai Chen, *The History of Chinese and Foreign Advertising* (in Chinese) (Beijing: China Wu Jia Press, 1997), p. 49.
54. Sherman Cochran, *Big Business in China: Sino-Foreign Rivalry in the Cigarette Industry, 1890-1930* (Cambridge, Mass.: Harvard University Press, 1980), p. 36.
55. Baiyi Xu, *Marketing to China: One Billion New Customers* (Lincolnwood, Ill.: NTC Business Books, 1990), p. xx.
56. *See* Sherman Cochran, *Big Business in China: Sino-Foreign Rivalry in the Cigarette Industry, 1890-1930* (Cambridge, Mass.: Harvard University Press, 1980).
57. Baiyi Xu, *Marketing to China: One Billion New Customers* (Lincolnwood, Ill.: NTC Business Books, 1990), p. xx.
58. Joint Economic Committee, Congress of the United States, *Chinese Economy Post-Mao*, vol. 1 (Washington, D.C.: U.S. Government Printing Office, 1978), p. 722.
59. *Statistical Yearbook of China* (various years) (Hong Kong: Hong Kong Economic Information and Agency).
60. Shanghai Academy of Social Sciences, *Shanghai Economy, 1949-1982* (in Chinese) (Shanghai: Shanghai People's Press, 1983), p. 623.
61. Pei-ai Chen, *The History of Chinese and Foreign Advertising* (in Chinese) (Beijing: China Wu Jia Press, 1997), p. 69.
62. Baiyi Xu, "Reaching the Chinese Consumer," *The China Business Review* (November/December 1992), pp. 36-42.
63. Shenming Huang, *An Empirical Analysis of Chinese Advertising* (in Chinese) (Beijing: Beijing Broadcast Institute Press, 1992), p. 13.

64. Pei-ai Chen, *The History of Chinese and Foreign Advertising* (in Chinese) (Beijing: China Wu Jia Press, 1997), p. 76.
65. James Chu, "Advertising in China: Its Policy, Practice and Evolution," *Journalism Quarterly* 59 (1982), p. 91.
66. *The History of the Development of Chinese Domestic Commerce and Industry* (in Chinese) (Heibei People's Press, 1997), p. 813.
67. Shenming Huang, *An Empirical Analysis of Chinese Advertising* (in Chinese) (Beijing: Beijing Broadcast Institute Press, 1992), p. 21.
68. Maurice M. Helain, "A Visit to the Canton Trade Fair," *The International Advertiser*, April 1966, p. 17.
69. *World Investment Report 1993: Transnational Corporation and Integrated International Production*, The United Nations Conference on Trade and Development Programme on Transnational Corporations.
70. Ibid.
71. *Business Week*, 8 July 1996, p. 46.
72. Richard Ohmann, ed., *Making and Selling Culture* (Hanover, Mass.: Wesleyan University Press, 1996), p. 4.
73. *Business Week*, 8 July 1996, p. 47.
74. *The New York Times*, 2 December 1996, p. C10.
75. *See* Al Hester, "Theoretical Considerations in Predicting Volume and Direction of International Information Flow," *Gazette* 19 (1973), pp. 239-247.
76. Armand Mattelart, *Advertising International: The Privatization of Public Sphere* (London: Routledge, 1991), p. 3.
77. *Advertising Age* (various years).
78. *The People's Daily*, overseas edition, 2 March 1995, p. 2.
79. Ibid.
80. *The People's Daily*, overseas edition, 14 October 1996, p. 2.
81. *The People's Daily*, overseas edition, 5 June 1996, p. 1.
82. *China Advertising*, January 1998, p. 14.
83. Nicholas R. Lardy, "The Role of Foreign Trade and Investment in China's Economic Reform," *The China Quarterly* 114 (1995), p. 1065.
84. *See* Michel Oksenberg and James Tong, "The Evolution of Central-provincial Fiscal Relations in China, 1971-1984," *The China Quarterly* 125 (1991), pp. 1-32.
85. Judy Polumbaum, "Between Propaganda and Junk-food Journalism: Exploratory Terrains in Mainland Chinese News Coverage,"

paper presented at the Annual Conference of the Association for Education in Journalism and Mass Communication, Atlanta, Georgia, U.S.A., 1994.

86. Ximin Zhang, "Chinese Newspaper Industry" and "Chinese Television Industry," in *The State and Trend of Development in China, 1996-1997* (in Chinese) (Beijing: The Chinese Academy of Social Sciences Press, 1996), pp. 286-323.
87. Ximin Zhang, "Press and Book Publishing Industry" and "Radio, TV and Video Industry," in *The State and Trend of Development in China, 1995-1996* (in Chinese) (Beijing: The Chinese Academy of Social Sciences Press, 1995), pp. 256-315.
88. Ximin Zhang, "Chinese Newspaper Industry" and "Chinese Television Industry," in *The State and Trend of Development in China, 1996-1997* (in Chinese) (Beijing: The Chinese Academy of Social Sciences Press, 1996), pp. 286-323.
89. Ximin Zhang, "Press and Book Publishing Industry" and "Radio, TV and Video Industry," in *The State and Trend of Development in China, 1995-1996* (in Chinese) (Beijing: The Chinese Academy of Social Sciences Press, 1995), pp. 256-315.
90. Ibid.
91. *The Wall Street Journal*, 28 September 1994, p. 81.
92. The Associated Press story, *The Daily Iowan*, 26 June 1996, p. 6.
93. Zhongdang Pan, "Improvising for Social Change: Interpreting China's Journalism Reform," paper presented at the Conference on Chinese Communication in the Age of Modern Media, University of Minnesota, U.S.A., 1996.
94. Quoted in Michael D. Rice, "China's Sleeping Ad Market Wakes Up," *Marketing News*, 25 September 1987, p. 4.
95. *China Advertising Yearbook 1994* (in Chinese) (Beijing: Xin Hua Press, 1995), p. 4.
96. Randall Stross, *Bulls in the China Shop and Other Sino-American Business Encounters* (New York: Pantheon Books, 1990), p. 229.
97. *The China Business Review*, May/June 1979, p. 38.
98. Shenming Huang, *An Empirical Analysis of Chinese Advertising* (in Chinese) (Beijing: Beijing Broadcast Institute Press, 1992), p. 28.
99. Xizhou Chen, "Some Thoughts on the Advertising Market under Development," in *China Advertising Yearbook 1994* (in Chinese) (Beijing: Xinhua Press, 1995), pp. 129-131.

100. Randall Stross, *Bulls in the China Shop and Other Sino-American Business Encounters* (New York: Pantheon Books, 1990), p. 239.
101. *Advertising Age*, 4 May 1987, p. 76.
102. Shenming Huang, *An Empirical Analysis of Chinese Advertising* (in Chinese) (Beijing: Beijing Broadcast Institute Press, 1992), p. 31.
103. *China Advertising Yearbook 1996* (in Chinese).
104. *China Advertising Yearbook 1994 and 1996* (in Chinese); *China Advertising* (in Chinese), March 1998, p. 12.
105. *See also Modern Advertising* (in Chinese), January 1997, pp. 38-39.
106. *China Advertising Yearbook 1994* (in Chinese), p. 10.
107. *Beijing Review*, 21-27 February 1994, p. 12.
108. *Advertising and Marketing in China: Past, Present and Future* (Hong Kong: The Asia Letter, 1985), pp. 313-322.
109. Michael H. Anderson, *Madison Avenue in Asia: Politics and Transnational Advertising* (London: Associated University Press, 1984), p. 271.
110. Scott D. Seligman, "China's Fledgling Advertising Industry: The Start of Something Big?" *The China Business Review*, January/February 1984, pp. 12-17.
111. Michael H. Anderson, *Madison Avenue in Asia: Politics and Transnational Advertising* (London: Associated University Press, 1984), p. 272.
112. Scott D. Seligman, "China's Fledgling Advertising Industry: The Start of Something Big?" *The China Business Review*, January/February 1984, pp. 12-17.
113. Ibid.
114. Michael D. Rice, "China's Sleeping Ad Market Wakes Up," *Marketing News*, 25 September 1987, p. 4.
115. J. Walter Thompson ad in *Asian Advertising and Marketing*, January 1987.
116. Leo Burnett ad in *Asian Advertising and Marketing*, January 1987.
117. *The Wall Street Journal*, 7 November 1991, p. A11.
118. *Advertising Age*, 4 June 1990, p. 41.
119. *Advertising Age*, 12 November 1990, p. 64.
120. *Advertising Age*, 21 August 1992, p. 12.
121. Thamis Lo and Amy Yung, "Multinational Service Firms in Centrally Planned Economies: Foreign Advertising Agencies in the PRC," *Marketing International Research* 28, no. 1 (1988), pp. 26-33.

122. Hong Cheng and Kathrine Frith, "Foreign Advertising Agencies in China," *Media Asia* 23, no. 1 (1996), pp. 34-41.
123. *South China Morning Post*, 27 September 1992, p. 3.
124. *Business Week*, 22 December 1997, p. 23.
125. *China Advertising*, January 1998, p. 14, and March 1998, p. 12.
126. *Media*, 6 August 1993.
127. Interview with a foreign ad executive, Beijing, 1996.

Chapter 3

1. Daniel Bell, *The Cultural Contradictions of Capitalism* (New York: Basic Books, 1976), p. 68.
2. Mary Douglas and Baron Isherwood, *The World of Goods: Towards an Anthropology of Consumption* (New York: Basic Books, 1979).
3. Jackson Lears, *Fables of Abundance: A Cultural History of Advertising in America* (New York: Basic Books, 1994), p. 3.
4. Leo Lee, "The Cultural Construction of Modernity in Print Journalism" (unpublished manuscript), p. 27.
5. Jib Fowles, *Advertising and Popular Culture* (Thousand Oaks, Calif.: Sage Publications, 1996), p. 167.
6. As exemplified by the classic study of a day in the world's prestige press directed by Wilbur Schramm in the 1950s and the more recent InterMedia TV news agenda survey, this type of snapshot study can yield revealing information about our everyday media environment. *See* Wilbur Schramm, *One Day in the World's Press: Fourteen Great Newspapers on a Day of Crisis, November 2, 1956* (Stanford, Calif.: Stanford University Press, 1956) and InterMedia, *The Global News Agenda* 20, nos. 1 and 2 (1992).
7. Francis Fukuyama, *The End of History and the Last Man* (New York: The Free Press, 1992), p. 126.
8. *Beijing Review*, 24 November 1980, p. 28.
9. *See* Raymond Williams, *Keywords* (New York: Oxford University Press, 1976), pp. 78-79.
10. *China Today*, North American edition, 5 May 1994, p. 10.
11. Daniel Bell, *The Cultural Contradictions of Capitalism* (New York: Basic Books, 1976), p. 68.
12. I surveyed six advertising vehicles: newspaper, magazine, TV, radio, outdoor billboard, and subway. The selection of the print and broadcast media was based on readership and viewer data compiled by the

Survey Research Group China (1995). The three most popular daily newspapers in Beijing were the *Beijing Evening News*, *Beijing Daily*, and *Beijing Youth Daily*; the most read weekly newspapers were *Beijing TV and Broadcast Guide* and *China TV Guide*. The *People's Daily* was also included in the survey primarily due to its national prominence. The three most popular monthly magazines were *The Reader*, *Youth Digest*, and *Popular Cinema*. The two most watched television channels in Beijing were China Central TV Channel 1 (CCTV1) and Beijing TV Channel 1 (BTV1). Only prime-time advertising was monitored. Beijing Music Radio was the most listened to FM station. This snapshot study surveyed three different time slots in the morning, afternoon, and evening. The site of outdoor billboards was Jian Guo Men Wai Avenue. With many office towers and billboards along the avenue, it is known as Beijing's corporate center. Fu Xin Men is one of the busiest subway stations, and this survey also included the panel posters that lined the walls of the station.

13. Sally Stewart and Nigel Campbell, "Advertising in Mainland China: A Preliminary Study," *International Journal of Advertising* 5 (1986), pp. 317-323.
14. Ibid.
15. For instance, advertising is regarded as a parable in Roland Marchand, *Advertising the American Dream: Making Way for Modernity, 1920-1940* (Berkeley: University of California Press, 1985) and a fable in Jackson Lears, *Fables of Abundance: A Cultural History of Advertising in America* (New York: Basic Books, 1994). A narrative has two dimensions: story (*histoire*) and discourse (*discours*). Story refers to the content of the narrative (e.g., events, actions, etc.), and discourse is the expression of the events and actions. *See* Seymour Chatman, *Story and Discourse: Narrative Structure in Fiction and Film* (Ithaca, N.Y.: Cornell University Press, 1978), p. 19.
16. Marshall Berman, *All That Is Solid Melts into Air: The Experience of Modernity* (New York: Penguin Books, 1982).
17. Anthony Giddens, *The Consequences of Modernity* (Stanford, Calif.: Stanford University Press, 1990), p. 1.
18. Daniel Bell, *The Cultural Contradictions of Capitalism* (New York: Basic Books, 1976), p. 46.
19. Russell W. Belk and Richard W. Pollay, "Images of Ourselves: The Good Life in Twentieth Century Advertising," *Journal of Consumer Research* 11 (1985), pp. 887-897.

20. Daniel Bell, *The Cultural Contradictions of Capitalism* (New York: Basic Books, 1976), p. 70.
21. Russell W. Belk, "Third World Consumer Culture," in *Research in Marketing Supplement 4*, ed. Erdogan Kumcu, (Greenwich, Conn.: JAI Press, 1988), pp. 113-128.
22. Ibid.
23. This part of the study is based on an analysis of foreign advertisements in two daily newspapers in China from 1985 to 1993: the *People's Daily* and *Wen Hui Bao*. For each paper, two weeks' issues in each of the four time periods (i.e., 1985-1986, 1987-1988, 1990-1991, and 1992-1993) were randomly selected. The unit of analysis is each advertisement in the sample (excluding exhibition notices, company announcements, and ads for publications, movies, and theater performances).
24. Paul Rutherford, *The New Icons? The Art of Television Advertising* (Toronto: University of Toronto Press, 1994), p. 124.
25. *China Statistical Yearbook 1993* (Beijing: China Statistical Bureau, 1994), p. 279.
26. Stuart Ewen, *Captains of Consciousness: Advertising and the Social Roots of the Consumer Culture* (New York: McGraw-Hill Book Company, 1976), p. 107.
27. Millie R. Creighton, "Imaging the Other in Japanese Advertising Campaigns," in *Occidentalism: Images of the West*, ed. James G. Carrier (Oxford: Clarendon Press, 1995), p. 135.
28. *See* Elli Lester, "Buying the Exotic 'Other': Reading the 'Banana Republic' Mail Order Catalog," *Journal of Communication Inquiry* 16, no. 2 (1992), pp. 74-85.
29. *See* "The Advertising Century," a special issue of *Advertising Age*, *http://www.adage.com/century*.
30. There were eight participants (four male and four female) in the focus group. The discussion took place in the school's faculty meeting room on a late afternoon after class. The session lasted one hour, and it was taped. There was much interaction among the participants during the session.
31. The campus survey was conducted in two classes at this vocational school with a total of 196 participants. Along with basic information about media use, the survey focused on attitudes toward foreign advertising.
32. Richard W. Pollay, David K. Tse, and Zhangyuan Wang, "Advertising, Propaganda, and Value Change in Economic Development: The

New Cultural Revolution in China and Attitudes Toward Advertising," *Journal of Business Research* 20 (1990), pp. 83-95.

33. Reported in Shenming Huang, *An Empirical Analysis of Chinese Advertising* (Beijing: Beijing Broadcast Institute Press, 1992), p. 183.
34. Ibid., p. 184.
35. Ibid.
36. Ibid., p. 186.
37. Randall Stross, *Bulls in the China Shop and Other Sino-American Business Encounters* (New York: Pantheon Books, 1990), p. 234. The only study that seems to present some contradictory indication about Chinese consumers' attitudes toward foreign advertising is a survey conducted in Beijing in 1987. *See* Xinshu Zhao and Fuyuan Shen, "Audience Reaction to Commercial Advertising in China in the 1980s," *International Journal of Advertising* 14 (1995), pp. 374-390. The research found that two-thirds of the Beijing residents preferred Chinese domestic ads to foreign ads. But the research did not provide any evidence or explanation as to why there was such a preference.

Chapter 4

1. *See* Wendy Griswold, *Cultures and Societies in a Changing World* (Thousand Oaks, Calif.: Pine Forge Press, 1994).
2. To protect the confidentiality of the sources, the pseudonym "Agency" is used for the agency under study. I spent a month at the Agency as a participant observer in spring 1996. The one-month stay was divided among the three departments, one week each in the account service and the creative department, and two weeks in the media department. I learned about the daily routines of the Agency through a variety of sources, including using direct observation, attending meetings, conducting formal and informal interviews, socializing with the staff (e.g., during lunch breaks), reading agency documents, and helping with projects.
3. Howard Becker, "Art as Collective Action," *American Sociological Review* 39, no. 6 (1974), p. 774.
4. *The New York Times*, 4 August 1996, p. H30.
5. Erdener Kaynak, *The Management of International Advertising: A Handbook and Guide for Professionals* (New York: Quorum Book, 1989), pp. 178-179.
6. Nei Fligstein, "Markets as Politics: A Political-cultural Approach to

Market Institutions," *American Sociological Review* 61 (August 1996), pp. 656-673.

7. Pitman B. Potter, "Foreign Investment Law in the People's Republic of China: Dilemmas of State Control," *The China Quarterly* 141 (March 1995), p. 163.
8. Clifford Geertz, "The Javanese Kijaji: The Changing Role of a Cultural Broker," *Comparative Studies in Society and History* 2, no. 2 (1960), pp. 228-249.
9. Dennis Hume Wrong, *Max Weber* (Englewood Cliffs, N.J.: Prentice-Hall, 1970), p. 26.
10. Matthias Kipping and Ove Bjarnar, "The Marshall Plan and the Transfer of US Management Models to Europe: An Introductory Framework," in *The Americanization of European Business: The Marshall Plan and the Transfer of U.S. Management Models*, ed. Matthias Kipping and Ove Bjarnar (London: Routledge, 1998), p. 7. *See also* Martin Kenny and Richard Florida, *Beyond Mass Production: The Japanese System and its Transfer to the U.S.* (New York: Oxford University Press, 1993).
11. Ibid., p. 8.

Chapter 5

1. *See* Raymond Vernon, *Sovereignty at Bay: The Multinational Spread of U.S. Enterprises* (New York: Columbia University Press, 1971); Patrick McGovern, "*Sovereignty at Bay* Revisited? Globalization, the Nation State and Labor," *Asia Pacific Business Review* 3, no. 3 (1997), pp. 161-167.
2. An example of the optimistic school is Kenichi Ohmae, *The Borderless World: Power and Strategy in the Interlinked Economy* (New York: Harper Business, 1990). For a pessimistic view, *see* Jerry Mander and Edward Goldsmith, eds., *The Case Against the Global Economy and For a Turn Toward the Local* (San Francisco: Sierra Club Books, 1996).
3. *Business Week*, 23 October 1995, p. 52.
4. A caveat is in order before the discussion. The concept of regulation in this discussion refers specifically to government policies. Certainly a broader understanding of "regulation" would entail the "more general sense of the reproduction of a particular pattern and order of signifying practices," and hence the study of regulation of the cultural industry consists of both cultural policy and cultural

politics. *See* Kenneth Thompson, ed., *Media and Cultural Regulation* (London: Sage Publications in association with Open University, 1997). In this particular context, we are only dealing with the policy dimension of the concept of regulation.

5. *See* Xuejun Yu, "Government Policies Toward Advertising in China," *Gazette* 48 (1991), pp. 17-30.
6. James Chu, "Advertising in China: Its Policy, Practice and Evolution," *Journalism Quarterly* 59 (Spring 1982), pp. 40-45, 91.
7. Xuejun Yu, "Government Policies Toward Advertising in China," *Gazette* 48 (1991), pp. 17-30.
8. *The Advertising Law of the People's Republic of China: A Practical Guide* (in Chinese) (Beijing: Red Flag Press, 1994), pp. 12-13.
9. Pitman B. Porter, "Foreign Investment Law in the People's Republic of China: Dilemmas of State Control," *The China Quarterly* 141 (1995), p. 167.
10. Arnold K. Weinstein summarized the concerns of host governments over the impact of foreign multinational businesses in eight respects: (1) foreign domination of local firms; (2) reduction of opportunity for local firms; (3) foreign interference in internal economic planning; (4) ability to avoid internal economic constraints; (5) creation of technological dependence; (6) extraterritorial interference by the foreign government; (7) negative balance of payments effects; and (8) unwanted cultural impact. *See* Arnold K. Weinstein, "The U.S. Multinational Advertising Agency and Public Policy," *Journal of Advertising* 6, no. 4 (1977), pp. 19-24. In the case of foreign advertising in China, it appears the most important issues are foreign domination of the industry and its cultural influence.
11. *See* Pitman B. Porter, "Foreign Investment Law in the People's Republic of China: Dilemmas of State Control," *The China Quarterly* 141 (1995), p. 163.
12. Paul W. Beamish, "The Characteristics of Joint Ventures in the People's Republic of China," *Journal of International Marketing* 1, no. 2 (1993), p. 32.
13. Ibid., p. 33.
14. William Leiss, Stephen Kline, and Sut Jhally, *Social Communication in Advertising* (New York: Routledge, 1990), p. 352.
15. *A Practical Handbook of Advertising in China* (in Chinese) (Beijing: China Development Press, 1995), p. 406.
16. *Modern Advertising* (in Chinese), no. 2, 1996, p. 1.

17. *Media*, 24 July 1998, p. 23.
18. *Advertising Age*, 30 September 1991, p. 30.
19. The structure of national regulation in China has four tiers: (1) laws enacted by the National People's Congress; (2) administrative codes stipulated by the State Council; (3) laws enacted by provincial people's congresses; and (4) rules and regulations issued by the ministries under the State Council. There are numerous rules and regulations concerning advertising in different provinces and cities. Mentioned here are only the four major regulations over the years.
20. *See also* Hong Cheng, "Advertising in China: A Socialist Experiment," in *Advertising in Asia: Communication, Culture and Consumption*, ed. Katherine T. Frith, pp. 90-94 (Ames: Iowa State University Press, 1996).
21. Stanley Lubman, "Introduction: The Future of Chinese Law," *The China Quarterly* 141 (1995), p. 2.
22. Ibid., p. 6.
23. Interview in Beijing, 1996.
24. *Media*, 24 July 1998, p. 23.
25. Susan Strange, "The Defective State," *Daedalus* 124, no. 2 (1995), p. 57.
26. James Chadwick, "Navigating Through China's New Advertising Law: The Role of Marketing Research," *International Journal of Advertising* 16, no. 4 (1997), p. 286.
27. Interview in Beijing, 1996.
28. James Chadwick, "Navigating Through China's New Advertising Law: The Role of Marketing Research," *International Journal of Advertising* 16, no. 4 (1997), p. 293.
29. *Media*, 24 July 1998, p. 23.
30. Pitman B. Porter, "Foreign Investment Law in the People's Republic of China: Dilemmas of State Control," *The China Quarterly* 141 (1995), pp. 167-168.
31. Vivien A. Schmidt, "The New World Order, Incorporated: The Rise of Business and the Decline of the Nation State," *Daedalus* 124, no. 2 (1995), p. 85.

Chapter 6

1. *Business Week*, 30 November 1998, p. 14.
2. Jan Nederveen Pieterse, "Globalization as Hybridization," in *Global Modernities*, ed. Mike Featherstone, Scott Lash, and Roland Robertson (Thousand Oaks, Calif.: Sage Publications, 1995), p. 53.

3. Malcolm Waters, *Key Ideas: Globalization* (London: Routledge, 1995), p. 3.
4. *See* George Ritzer, *The McDonaldization of Society: An Investigation into the Changing Character of Contemporary Social Life* (Thousand Oaks, Calif.: Pine Forge Press, 1996).
5. Arif Dirlik, "The Global in the Local," in *Global/Local: Cultural Production and the Transnational Imaginary*, ed. Rob Wilson and Wilmal Dissanayake (Durham, N.C.: Duke University Press, 1996), p. 23.
6. Benjamin R. Barber, *Jihad vs. McWorld: How Globalism and Tribalism Are Reshaping the World* (New York: Ballantine Books, 1995), p. 157.
7. Jan Nederveen Pieterse, "Globalization as Hybridization," in *Global Modernities*, ed. Mike Featherstone, Scott Lash, and Roland Robertson (Thousand Oaks, Calif.: Sage Publications, 1995).
8. Jonathan Friedman, "Global System, Globalization and the Prarmeters of Modernity," in *Global Modernities*, ed. Mike Featherstone, Scott Lash, and Roland Robertson (Thousand Oaks, Calif.: Sage Publications, 1995), p. 78.
9. Ibid.
10. *See*, for instance, Tamar Liebes and Elihu Katz, *The Export of Meaning: Cross-Cultural Readings of* Dallas (New York: Oxford University Press, 1990).
11. Baiyi Xu, *Marketing to China: One Billion New Customers* (Lincolnwood, Ill.: NTC Business, 1990), p. 31.
12. *See A Practical Handbook of Advertising in China* (Beijing: China Development Publishing House, 1995), p. 1. (in Chinese)
13. *See*, for instance, George E. Belch and Michael A. Belch, *Introduction to Advertising and Promotion: An Integrated Marketing Communications Perspective,* 3rd edition (Chicago: Richard D. Irwin, Inc., 1995), p. 11.
14. Randall Stross, *Bulls in the China Shop and Other Sino-American Business Encounters* (New York: Pantheon Books, 1990), p. 240.
15. Jeremy Tunstall, *The Media Are American* (New York: Columbia University Press, 1977), p. 63.
16. As Stephen Kalberg pointed out, "To the degree that sheer calculation in terms of abstract rule reigns, decisions are arrived at 'without regard to persons.' An orientation of action to formal rules and laws is tantamount to a rejection of all arbitrariness: universalism and calculation in reference to enacted regulations stand here

strictly opposed to decision making in reference to the personal qualities of individuals concerned." Stephen Kalberg, "Max Weber's Types of Rationality: Cornerstones for the Analysis of Rationalization Processes in History," *American Journal of Sociology* 85, no. 5 (1980), p. 1158.

17. Paul W. Beamish, "The Characteristics of Joint Ventures in the People's Republic of China," *Journal of International Marketing* 1, no. 2 (1993), p. 39.
18. Interviews with Baiyi Xu in Shanghai, 1996.
19. Carl Crow, *My Friends, The Chinese* (London: Hamish Hamilton, 1938), p. 169.
20. Sandra E. Moriarty and Thomas R. Duncan, "Global Advertising: Issues and Practices," *Current Issues and Research in Advertising* 13, no. 2 (1991), p. 333.
21. Sherman Cochran, *Big Business in China: Sino-Foreign Rivalry in the Cigarette Industry, 1890-1930* (Cambridge, Mass.: Harvard University Press, 1980), p. 35.
22. Ibid., p. 36.
23. Theodore Levitt, "The Globalization of Markets," *Harvard Business Review*, May/June 1983, p. 102.
24. Susan P. Douglas and Yoram Wind, "The Myth of Globalization," *The Columbia Journal of World Business* 22, Winter (1987), pp. 19-29.
25. Anthony Giddens, *The Consequences of Modernity* (Stanford, Calif.: Stanford University Press, 1990), p. 175.
26. Michael Schudson, *Advertising, The Uneasy Persuasion: Its Dubious Impact on American Society* (New York: Basic Books, 1984), p. 151.
27. Roland Marchand, *Advertising the American Dream: Making Way for Modernity, 1920-1940* (Berkeley: University of California Press, 1985), p. 218.
28. For a discussion of the deleterious impact of consumer advertising, *see* Christopher Lasch, *The Culture of Narcissism: American Life in an Age of Diminishing Expectations* (New York: W.W. Norton and Company, 1978), pp. 71-77.
29. *See* Jian Wang and Tsan-Kuo Chang, "From Class Ideologies to State Manager: TV Programming and Foreign Imports," *Journal of Broadcasting and Electronic Media* 40 (1996), pp. 196-207.
30. Randall Stross, "The Return of Advertising in China: A Survey of

the Ideological Reversal," *The China Quarterly* 123 (1990), pp. 494-495.

31. Two more aspects of foreign advertising that deserve our attention were not part of this project. One deals with the role of foreign advertising in the commercialization of the Chinese media. The other topic is related to the impact of foreign advertising on the market condition in China.

Epilogue

1. *South China Morning Post*, 1 August 1999, Business section, p. 3.
2. Jim Ayala and Richard Lai, "China's Consumer Market: A Huge Opportunity to Fail?" *The McKinsey Quarterly* (1996), no. 3, p. 57. *See also* Conghua Li, *China: The Consumer Revolution* (Singapore: John Wiley and Sons, 1998).
3. Scott D. Seligman, "China's Fledgling Advertising Industry: The Start of Something Big?" *The China Business Review,* January/February 1984, p. 17.
4. *Media* (Chinese edition), January/February 1999, p. 1.
5. *South China Morning Post*, 1 August 1999, Business section, p. 3.
6. C.K. Prahalad and Kenneth Lieberthal, "The End of Corporate Imperialism," *Harvard Business Review*, July/August 1998, p. 70.
7. *Media*, 28 May 1999, p. 1.
8. Jeffrey E. Garten, "Opening the Doors for Business in China," *Harvard Business Review*, May/June 1998, p. 167.
9. Carl Crow, *Foreign Devils in the Flowery Kingdom* (New York: Harpers and Brothers, 1940), pp. 327-328.
10. Ibid., p. 328.

Selected Bibliography

Advertising and Marketing in China: Past, Present and Future. Hong Kong: The Asia Letter, 1985.

The Advertising Law of the People's Republic of China: A Practical Guide. Beijing: Red Flag Press, 1994. (in Chinese)

Anderson, Michael H. *Madison Avenue in Asia: Politics and Transnational Advertising*. London: Associated University Press, 1984.

Appadurai, Arjun. "Disjuncture and Difference in the Global Cultural Economy." *Theory, Culture and Society* 7 (1990): 295-310.

______. *Modernity at Large: Cultural Dimensions of Globalization*. Minneapolis: University of Minnesota Press, 1996.

Ayish, Muhammadi. "International Communication in the 1990s: Implications for the Third World." *International Affairs* 68, no. 3 (1992): 487-510.

Barber, Benjamin R. *Jihad vs. McWorld: How Globalism and Tribalism Are Reshaping the World*. New York: Ballantine Books, 1995.

Barnet, Richard J., and John Cavanagh. *The Global Dreams: Imperial Corporations and the New World Order*. New York: Touchstone, 1994.

Barnet, Richard J., and Ronald E. Muller. *Global Reach: The Power of the Multinational Corporations*. New York: Simon and Schuster, 1974.

Beamish, Paul W. "The Characteristics of Joint Ventures in the People's Republic of China." *Journal of International Marketing* 1, no. 2 (1993): 29-48.

Belk, Russell W. "Third World Consumer Culture." In *Research in Marketing Supplement 4*, edited by Erdogan Kumcu, 113-128. Greenwich, Conn.: JAI Press, 1988.

Belk, Russell W., and Richard W. Pollay. "Images of Ourselves: The Good Life in Twentieth Century Advertising." *Journal of Consumer Research* 11 (1985): 887-897.

Bell, Daniel. *The Cultural Contradictions of Capitalism.* New York: Basic Books, 1976.

Berman, Marshall. *All That Is Solid Melts into Air: The Experience of Modernity.* New York: Penguin Books, 1982.

Biltereyst, Daniel. "Qualitative Audience Research and Transnational Media Effects: A New Paradigm?" *European Journal of Communication* 10, no. 2 (1995): 245-270.

Bocock, Robert. *Key Ideas: Consumption.* London: Routledge, 1993.

Boyd-Barrett, Oliver. "Media Imperialism: Towards an International Framework for the Analysis of Media System." In *Mass Communication and Society*, edited by James Curran, Michael Gurevitch and Janet Woollacott, 116-141. Thousand Oaks, Calif.: Sage Publications, 1979.

Buell, Frederick. *National Culture and the New Global System.* Baltimore, Md.: The Johns Hopkins University Press, 1993.

Chen, Pei-ai. *The History of Chinese and Foreign Advertising.* Beijing: China Wu Jia Press, 1997. (in Chinese)

Chen, Xiaomei. *Occidentalism: A Theory of Counter-Discourse in Post-Mao China.* New York: Oxford University Press, 1995.

Cheng, Hong. "Advertising in China: A Socialist Experiment." In *Advertising in Asia: Communication, Culture and Consumption*, edited by Katherine T. Frith, 90-94. Ames: Iowa State University Press, 1996.

Cheng, Hong, and Kathrine Frith. "Foreign Advertising Agencies in China." *Media Asia* 23, no. 1 (1996): 34-41.

China Advertising Yearbook 1994. Beijing: Xin Hua Press, 1995. (in Chinese)

China Advertising Yearbook 1996. Beijing: Xin Hua Press, 1997. (in Chinese)

Chu, James. "Advertising in China: Its Policy, Practice and Evolution." *Journalism Quarterly* 59 (1982): 40-45, 91.

Cochran, Sherman. *Big Business in China: Sino-Foreign Rivalry in the Cigarette Industry, 1890-1930.* Cambridge, Mass.: Harvard University Press, 1980.

Creighton, Millie R. "Imaging the Other in Japanese Advertising Campaigns." In *Occidentalism: Images of the West*, edited by James G. Carrier, 135-160. Oxford: Clarendon Press, 1995.

Crow, Carl. *Four Hundred Million Customers: The Friendly Chinaman and His Business.* New York: Harpers and Brothers, 1937.

_____. *Newspaper Directory of China.* Shanghai: Carl Crow, Inc., 1937.

_____. *My Friends, The Chinese.* London: Hamish Hamilton, 1938.

_____. *Foreign Devils in the Flowery Kingdom.* New York: Harpers and Brothers, 1940.

Dernberger, Robert. "The Role of Foreigner in China's Economic Development, 1840-1949." In *China's Modern Economy in Historical Perspective*, edited by Dwight H. Perkins, 19-47. Stanford, Calif.: Stanford University Press, 1975.

Dirlik, Arif. "The Global in the Local." In *Global/Local: Cultural Production and the Transnational Imaginary*, edited by Rob Wilson and Wimal Dissanayake, 21-45. Durham, N.C.: Duke University Press, 1996.

Doremus, Paul N., William W. Keller, Louis W. Pauly, and Simon Reich. *The Myth of the Global Corporation.* Princeton, N.J.: Princeton University Press, 1998.

Dorfman, Ariel, and Armand Mattelart. *How to Read Donald Duck: Imperialist Ideology in the Disney Comic*, translated by D. Kunzle. New York: International General Editions, 1975.

Douglas, Mary, and Baron Isherwood. *The World of Goods: Towards an Anthropology of Consumption.* New York: Basic Books, 1979.

Douglas, Susan P., and Yoram Wind. "The Myth of Globalization." *The Columbia Journal of World Business* 22, Winter (1987): 19-29.

Ewen, Stuart. *Captains of Consciousness: Advertising and the Social Roots of the Consumer Culture.* New York: McGraw-Hill Book Company, 1976.

Fairbank, John K. *The United States and China*, 4th ed. Cambridge, Mass.: Harvard University Press, 1979.

Featherstone, Mike. "Localism, Globalism, and Cultural Identity." In *Global/Local: Cultural Production and the Transnational Imaginary*, edited by Rob Wilson and Wimal Dissanayake, 47-77. Durham, N.C.: Duke University Press, 1996.

Fejes, Fred. "The Growth of Multinational Advertising Agencies in Latin America." *Journal of Communication* 30, no. 3 (1980): 36-49.

_____. "Media Imperialism: An Assessment," *Media, Culture and Society (*1981): 345-353.

Feuerwerker, Albert. *The Foreign Establishment in China in the Early Twentieth Century.* Ann Arbor: Center for Chinese Studies at the University of Michigan, 1976.

______. *The Chinese Economy, 1870-1949.* Ann Arbor: Center for Chinese Studies at the University of Michigan, 1995.

Fowles, Jib. *Advertising and Popular Culture.* Thousand Oaks, Calif.: Sage Publications, 1996.

Fox, Stephen. *The Mirror Makers: A History of American Advertising and Its Creators.* New York: Vintage Books, 1985.

Frazer, Charles F. "Issues and Evidence in International Advertising." *Current Issues and Research in Advertising* 12, no. 1 (1990): 75-90.

Friedman, Jonathan. "Being in the World: Globalization and Localization." *Theory, Culture and Society* 7 (1990): 311-328.

______. "Global System, Globalization and the Parameters of Modernity." In Mike Featherstone, Scott Lash, and Roland Robertson (ed.) *Global Modernities,* 69-90. Thousand Oaks, Calif.: Sage Publications, 1995.

Frith, Katherine T., and Michael Frith. "Advertising as Cultural Invasion," *Media Asia* 16, no. 4 (1989): 179-184, 214.

______. "Western Advertising and Eastern Culture: The Confrontation in Southeast Asia," *Current Issues and Research in Advertising* 12, no. 1 (1990): 63-73.

Ge, Gongzhen. *The History of Chinese Newspapers.* Hong Kong: Taiping Press, 1964. (in Chinese)

Giddens, Anthony. *The Consequences of Modernity.* Stanford, Calif.: Stanford University Press, 1990.

"Global Adspend Trends." *International Journal of Advertising* 17, 255-262. 1998.

Goffman, Erving. *Gender Advertisements.* Cambridge, Mass.: Harvard University Press, 1979.

Greider, Willliam. *One World, Ready or Not: The Manic Logic of Global Capitalism.* New York: Touchstone, 1997.

Griswold, Wendy. *Cultures and Societies in a Changing World.* Thousand Oaks, Calif.: Pine Forge Press, 1994.

Hamelink, Cees J. *Cultural Autonomy in Global Communication: Planning National Information Policy.* New York: Longman, 1983.

Hou, Chi-ming. *Foreign Investment and Economic Development in China, 1840-1937.* Cambridge, Mass.: Harvard University Press, 1965.

Hower, Ralph M. *The Story of an Advertising Agency: N.W. Ayer & Son at Work*. Cambridge, Mass.: Harvard University Press, 1939.

Huang, Shenming. *An Empirical Analysis of Chinese Advertising*. Beijing: Beijing Broadcast Institute Press, 1992. (in Chinese)

International Commission for the Study of Communication Problems (The MacBride Report), *Many Voices, One World: Towards a New More Just and More Efficient World Information and Communication Order*. UNESCO, 1980.

Janus, Noreene Z. "Advertising and the Mass Media in the Era of the Global Corporation." In *Communication and Social Structure: Critical Studies in Mass Media Research,* edited by Emile G. McAnany, Jorge Schritman, and Noreene Z. Janus, 287-316. New York: Praegers, 1981.

_____. "Advertising and the Mass Media: Transnational Link Between Production and Consumption." *Media Culture and Society* 3 (1981): 13-23.

Kaynak, Erdener. *The Management of International Advertising: A Handbook and Guide for Professionals*. New York: Quorum Book, 1989.

Kenny, Martin, and Richard Florida. *Beyond Mass Production: The Japanese System and its Transfer to the U.S.* New York: Oxford University Press, 1993.

Kim, Kwangmi K. "Spreading the Net: The Consolidation Process of Large Transnational Advertising Agencies in the 1980s and Early 1990s." *International Journal of Advertising* 14(1995): 195-217.

Kim, Kwangmi K., and Katherine Frith. "An Analysis of the Growth of Transnational Advertising in Five Asian Countries: 1970—1990." *Media Asia* 20, no. 1 (1993): 45-53, 56.

Kipping, Matthias, and Ove Bjarnar. *The Americanization of European Business: The Marshall Plan and the Transfer of U.S. Management Models*. London: Routledge, 1998.

Lardy, Nicholas R. "The Role of Foreign Trade and Investment in China's Economic Reform." *The China Quarterly* 114 (1995): 1065-1082.

Lasch, Christopher. *The Culture of Narcissism: American Life in an Age of Diminishing Expectations*. New York: W.W. Norton and Company, 1978.

Lears, Jackson. *Fables of Abundance: A Cultural History of Advertising in America*. New York: Basic Books, 1994.

Lee, Chin-chuan. *Media Imperialism Reconsidered: The Homogenizing of Television Culture.* Beverly Hills, Calif.: Sage Publications, 1980.

Leiss, William, Stephen Kline, and Sut Jhally. *Social Communication in Advertising.* New York: Routledge, 1990.

Lerner, Daniel. *The Passing of Traditional Society.* New York: Macmillan, 1958.

Levine, Lawrence W. *The Opening of the American Mind: Canons, Cultures and History.* Boston: Beacon Press, 1996.

Levitt, Theodore. "The Globalization of Markets." *Harvard Business Review*, May/June 1983: 92-102.

Li, Conghua. *China: The Consumer Revolution.* Singapore: John Wiley and Sons, 1998.

Li, Dong, and Alec. M. Gallup. "In Search of the Chinese Consumer." *The China Business Review* (September/October 1995): 19-22.

Liebes, Tamar ,and Elihu Katz. *The Export of Meaning: Cross-Cultural Readings of Dallas.* New York: Oxford University Press, 1990.

Lo, Thamis, and Amy Yung. "Multinational Service Firms in Centrally Planned Economies: Foreign Advertising Agencies in the PRC." *Marketing International Research* 28, no. 1 (1988): 26-33.

Mander, Jerry, and Edward Goldsmith (eds.). *The Case Against the Global Economy and for a Turn Toward the Local.* San Francisco: Sierra Club Books, 1996.

Marchand, Roland. *Advertising the American Dream: Making Way for Modernity, 1920-1940.* Berkeley: University of California Press, 1985.

Mattelart, Armand. *Multinational Corporations and the Control of Culture: The Ideological Apparatus of Imperialism.* Atlantic Highlands, N.J.: Humanities Press, 1979.

______. *Advertising International: The Privatization of Public Sphere.* London: Routledge, 1991.

McGovern, Patrick. "*Sovereignty at Bay* Revisited? Globalization, the Nation State and Labor." *Asia Pacific Business Review* 3, no. 3 (1997): 161-167.

Moriarty, Sandra E., and Thomas R. Duncan. "Global Advertising: Issues and Practices." *Current Issues and Research in Advertising* 13, no. 2 (1991): 313-341.

Nordenstreng, Kaarle, and Herbert I. Schiller (eds.). *National Sovereignty and International Communication.* Norwood, N.J.: Ablex Publishing, 1979.

Ohmae, Kenichi. *The Borderless World: Power and Strategy in the Interlinked Economy.* New York: Harper Business, 1990.

Ohmann, Richard (ed.). *Making and Selling Culture.* Hanover, N.H.: Wesleyan University Press, 1996.

Petras, James. "Cultural Imperialism in the Late 20th Century." *Journal of Contemporary Asia* 23, no. 2 (1993): 139-148.

Pieterse, Jan Nederveen. "Globalization as Hybridization." In *Global Modernities*, edited by Mike Featherstone, Scott Lash, and Roland Robertson, 45-68. Thousand Oaks, Calif.: Sage Publications, 1995.

Pollay, Richard W., David K. Tse, and Zhangyuan Wang. "Advertising, Propaganda, and Value Change in Economic Development: The New Cultural Revolution in China and Attitudes Toward Advertising." *Journal of Business Research* 20 (1990): 83-95.

Pope, Daniel. *The Making of Modern Advertising.* New York: Basic Books, 1983.

Porter, Pitman B. "Foreign Investment Law in the People's Republic of China: Dilemmas of State Control." *The China Quarterly* 141 (1995): 155-185.

Ritzer, George. *The McDonalization of Society: An Investigation into the Changing Character of Contemporary Social Life.* Thousand Oaks, Calif.: Pine Forge Press, 1996.

Robertson, Roland. "Glocalization: Time-space and Homogeneity-heterogeneity." In *Global Modernities*, edited by Mike Featherstone, Scott Lash, and Roland Robertson, 25-44. Thousand Oaks, Calif.: Sage Publications, 1995.

Said, Edward. *Culture and Imperialism.* New York: Vintage Books, 1993.

Salwen, Michael B. "Cultural Imperialism: A Media Effects Approach," *Critical Studies in Mass Communication* 8 (1991): 29-38.

Schell, Orville. *To Get Rich Is Glorious: China in the Eighties.* New York: Pantheon Books, 1984.

Schiller, Herbert I. *Mass Communication and American Empire.* New York: Augustus M. Kelley Publishers, 1969.

______. "Madison Avenue imperialism." In *Communication in International Politics*, edited by Richard L. Merritt, 318-339. Ill.: University of Illinois Press, 1972.

______. "Not Yet the Post-imperialist Era." *Critical Studies in Mass Communication* 8 (1991): 13-28.

Schmidt, Vivien A. "The New World Order, Incorporated: The Rise of Business and the Decline of the Nation State." *Daedalus* 124, no. 2 (1995): 75-106.

Schramm, Wilbur. *Mass Media and National Development.* Stanford, Calif.: Stanford University Press, 1964.

Schudson, Michael. *Advertising, The Uneasy Persuasion: Its Dubious Impact on American Society.* New York: Basic Books, 1984.

Seligman, Scott D. "China's Fledgling Advertising Industry: The Start of Something Big?" *The China Business Review* (January/February 1984): 12-17.

Sengupta, Subir, and Katherine Frith. "Multinational Corporation Advertising and Cultural Imperialism: A Content Analysis of Indian Television Commercials." *Asian Journal of Communication* 7, no. 1 (1997): 1-18.

Spence, Jonathan D. *The Search for Modern China.* New York: W.W. Norton and Company, 1990.

Stewart, Sally, and Nigel Campbell. "Advertising in Mainland China: A Preliminary Study." *International Journal of Advertising* 5 (1986): 317-323.

Strange, Susan. "The Defective State." *Daedalus* 124, no. 2 (1995): 55-74.

Straubhaar, Joseph D. "Beyond Media Imperialism: Asymmetrical Interdependence and Cultural Proximity," *Critical Studies in Mass Communication* 8 (1991): 39-59.

Stross, Randall. *Bulls in the China Shop and Other Sino-American Business Encounters.* New York: Pantheon Books, 1990.

Thompson, John B. *The Media and Modernity: A Social Theory of the Media.* Stanford, Calif.: Stanford University Press, 1995.

Thurow, Lester G. *The Future of Capitalism: How Today's Economic Forces Shape Tomorrow's World.* New York: William Morrow and Company, 1996.

Tomlinson, John. *Cultural Imperialism: A Critical Introduction*, 2nd ed. Baltimore, Md.: The Johns Hopkins University Press, 1992.

Tunstall, Jeremy. *The Advertising Man.* London: Chapman and Hall Ltd., 1964.

______. *The Media Are American.* New York: Columbia University Press, 1977.

Twitchell, James B. *Adcult USA: The Triumph of Advertising in American Culture.* New York: Columbia University Press, 1996.

Vernon, Raymond. *Sovereignty at Bay: The Multinational Spread of U.S. Enterprises.* New York: Columbia University Press, 1971.

Waters, Malcolm. *Key Ideas: Globalization.* London: Routledge, 1995.

Weinstein, Arnold K. "The U.S. Multinational Advertising Agency and Public Policy." *Journal of Advertising* 6, no. 4 (1977): 19-24.

Williams, Raymond. "Advertising: The Magic System." In *Problems in Materialism and Culture,* 170-195. London: Verso, 1980.

Xu, Baiyi. *Marketing to China: One Billion New Customers.* Lincolnwood, Ill.: NTC Business Books, 1990.

______. "Reaching the Chinese Consumer." *The China Business Review,* November/December 1992: 36-42.

______. "The Development of Advertising in Old Shanghai." In *Advertisements in the Old Time Shanghai.* Shanghai: Shanghai Pictorial Press, 1995. (in Chinese)

Young, Robert. *Colonial Desires: Hybridity in Theory, Culture and Race.* London: Routledge, 1995.

Yu, Xuejun. "Government Policies Toward Advertising in China." *Gazette* 48 (1991): 17-30.

Zhang, Ximin. "Press and Book Publishing Industry" and "Radio, TV and Video Industry." In *The State and Trend of Development in China, 1995-1996,* 256-315. Beijing: The Chinese Academy of Social Sciences Press, 1995. (in Chinese)

______. "Chinese Newspaper Industry" and "Chinese Television Industry." In *The State and Trend of Development in China, 1996-1997,* 286-323. Beijing: The Chinese Academy of Social Sciences Press, 1996. (in Chinese)

Zhao, Bin, and Graham Murdock, "Young Pioneers: Children and the Making of Chinese Consumerism." *Cultural Studies* 10 (1996), no. 2, 201-217.

Index

www.ingramcontent.com/pod-product-compliance
Ingram Content Group UK Ltd.
Pitfield, Milton Keynes, MK11 3LW, UK
UKHW020820290926
15470UKWH00003B/1284

9 780813 818283